Secret Societies

Other titles by this author

Urban Legends

Secret Societies

NICK HARDING

CHARTWELL
BOOKS, INC.

This edition published in 2006 by
CHARTWELL BOOKS, INC.
A division of BOOK SALES, INC.
114 Northfield Avenue
Edison, New Jersey 08837
USA

© Nick Harding 2005

The right of Nick Harding to be identified as author of this work has been asserted in accordance with the Copyright, Designs and Patents Act 1988

All rights reserved. No part of this book may be reproduced, stored in or introduced into a retrieval system, or transmitted, in any form or by any means (electronic, mechanical, photocopying, recording or otherwise) without the written permission of the publishers.

Any person who does any unauthorised act in relation to this publication may be liable to criminal prosecution and civil claims for damages.

A CIP catalogue record for this book is available from the Library of Congress.

ISBN 10: 0 7858 2170 8
ISBN 13: 978 0 7858 2170 0

2 4 6 8 10 9 7 5 3

Typeset by Avocet Typeset, Chilton, Aylesbury, Bucks, United Kingdom
Printed in the United States of America

Dedicated to the memory of Steve Redwood
Who fell too soon on his journey ... You will be missed.

For XTC and their music, thank you boys. Carl Sagan, Richard Dawkins, Michael Shermer and James Randi for showing the way in this demon-haunted world. Mo for just being her. Mike Gutsell and our reunion pint in the Dolphin and to Sean Martin who was a fellow witness to the exploding toilet in Cannes. I would also like to thank Nick Rennison for his alchemical skills with the text.

Contents

CONTENTS

Introduction

'Entre nous, c'est qu'on apelle
Le secret de Polichinelle'
La Mascotte, II, 12

Secret societies have existed in human society for thousands of years. In a sense the term 'secret society' is something of a misnomer as they are often very much in the public eye. In reality they are societies with apparent secrets and nothing more but it is often those supposed 'secrets' that garner the most attention. What troubles the majority of people is the presumed social effect these organisations have and their relationship to the democratic process. But are such anxieties justified? Are the Freemasons really running the world? If they are, how does this fit into the way the Bilderberg Group see things? Is the idea of a New World Order something on the agenda for the Skull and Bones or is it the sole *raison d'être* for the Illuminati? Do they all want to rule the world? If so, is there a hidden, worldwide war underway with each secret society vying for position with the others? Secret societies are illegal in several countries. In the European Union for example, Poland has made the ban a part of its constitution. Are they right to do so? Do these predominantly male-only organisations really crave world domination? Are they manipulating the media and brainwashing the populations of the world? Or are they just private clubs in which like-minded men can congregate together to relax and enjoy a convivial evening in each other's company?

Undoubtedly the desire to be part of some social elite, something that all humans feel at some time in their lives, is at work here. There is a desire to be separate from the 'ordinary' masses or to be part of something special, linked to the belief that becoming a member of an elite will bestow rich rewards, fiscal or otherwise. One criticism levelled at the Freemasons, for example, is that it is a business club in which deals are struck and a policy of 'you scratch my back, I'll scratch your back' is the rule. Yet, if this is the main objection to them, why is this criticism not aimed at an organisation such as the Lions club? This is not 'secret' but its members will, like the Freemasons, go out of their way to assist each other. Is that not what all groups do? What is it about the Freemasons and other secret societies that arouses the wrath of outsiders and distinguishes them from other social groupings?

All claim to hold secret knowledge that no one else does. All claim to be the holders of some form of truth. All claim to be the 'chosen' while considering all non-members, the laity, as outsiders and heathens who are ignorant and, in some cases, blind to 'reality'. All have initiation ceremonies, from the sublime to the alarming, that allow the acolyte to feel that they have entered something special. There is a purification element to these ceremonies in which the old world is 'washed away' and a new world entered. In this new world the new member can become party to the secret wisdom – the only secret wisdom worth knowing.

Often this so-called secret wisdom is just a way to secure the attentions of the newly recruited – a means of confounding the senses, promoting devotion and demanding the attentions of the acolyte. The Knights Templar were rumoured to know the whereabouts of the treasure of the Temple of Solomon and were alleged to be protecting the secret of the Holy Grail. The reality was less startling but the lure of the unknown is what makes these secret orders psychologically appealing. Perhaps, people think, even more arcane knowledge and more dramatic information that may surprise, anger, alarm or even amaze – depending on one's point of view or religious persuasion – may be in the hands of these orders. The classic 'secret' of this kind – popularised through such books as Lincoln, Baigent and Leigh's *The Holy Blood and the Holy Grail* and Dan Brown's *The DaVinci Code* – is that Jesus did not die on the cross and that Mary Magdalene, his wife, moved to the south of France, carrying his child.

Of course, these aspects of the secret societies based on Judao-Christian beliefs will be more predominant in Europe, the Middle East and North America. Elsewhere in the world such stories will have little or no meaning. The Tongs, for instance, have their secrets but they do not involve the activities of Jesus Christ and any family he may or may not have established in ancient Gaul.

With a secret society the element of control and an ingrained idea of power are always present. In many respects the 'secrets' they hold are nothing more than the window dressing for the outside world of the 'profane', intended to disguise this drive towards power and control. What secret societies deliberately do is develop an aura of mystique. They promote an 'us' and 'them', 'enlightened' and 'heathen' distinction. In their eyes, it is not so much that 'knowledge is power' as that 'hidden knowledge is power'. Whether that hidden knowledge is legitimate or not is always open to debate but, in the majority of cases, it tends to be empty and vacuous.

If knowledge is power, then secret knowledge is more powerful still. For example, shamans and 'cunning' women (witches) all had secrets in Bronze Age culture. Blacksmiths were people with great hidden knowledge, who were often relegated to the edge of their communities, but their skills were always sought out and deeply respected. In these instances, though, there were real quantifiable elements to their power. Blacksmiths had an intimate knowledge of metal working. 'Cunning' women understood the healing potential in the natural world. Both had secrets that were very much of the real world. Can secret societies boast the same?

What defines a secret society? B'nai B'rith, for example, is generally considered to be one but is it? Is it a just a worldwide organisation for the Jewish community or does it, as some on the Christian right would have us believe, have a sinister agenda? The fact is that, despite the criticisms, B'nai B'rith is nothing more than a communal organisation founded in New York by twelve German immigrants in 1843. Does the Bilderberg Group define economic strategy behind closed doors for a ruling right-wing elite, as some on the left believe? If so, why are parties of all political colours represented at its meetings? How do these myths develop? How is it that perfectly innocent organisations are assumed to be indulging in all kinds of lurid activities?

Are these misperceptions the fault of the societies themselves or a consequence of the way we view them? Do they act as a vehicle for our own fears and misgivings? If we feel that things are always against us, it is only too easy to believe that there is something working behind the scenes, some hidden cadre, to repress and oppress us. It is often our own fears that give weight to the perceived power of secret societies and, in many ways, the societies themselves are guilty of playing on those fears. Secret societies and the powers we ascribe to them reflect very human anxieties about control and repression.

Most critics of secret societies tend to be of the religious right who see all kinds of ungodly activities threatening their Christian ideologies. Activities within the hallowed walls of lodges, temples and sanctum sanctorums are often assumed to be the work of the Devil or Satan. In Ron Jonson's excellent *The Secret Rulers of the World* it is paranoid Christians who think the fall of society is imminent because of the 'nefarious' activities of these secret organisations. The old nonsense of the worldwide Jewish Conspiracy – that secret societies are the work of Zion hell-bent on bringing down all that is godfearing and sacred – is also thrown into the mix. However, the left also has its own agenda and often accuses Freemasonry, Bilderberg or 'The Bohemian Grove' of being undemocratic, elitist and essentially right-wing organisations which bypass the law of government and strive to establish a New World Order.

The overall appeal of membership of a secret society is that it allows the recruit to feel special, a part of a distinct elite, separate from the common herd. In a sense, entering a secret society is not that dissimilar an experience from building a den in childhood or joining a gang whose other members, more often than not, want the proposed new acolyte to engage in some dare, some 'baptism' of worthiness, to earn their respect. To be part of an elite group, a minority, is a very human desire, particularly in the male of the species. Social structures such as the golf club show that clearly enough. Advertising companies play on this all the time. Be part of something special, they urge, be different, have something that someone else doesn't have.

The other great myth of secret societies is that they possess 'The Secret' or 'Secrets'. In reality what can these all-embracing secrets be? One frequently repeated secret is, as mentioned earlier, that Jesus (Yehoshua ben Joseph, to give him his more likely name) either survived the cross or was not crucified at all and that he went on to marry Mary and to father children. Can that be described as a secret? Or is it just a possibility, which might or might not be historically accurate? The only genuine 'secrets' that exist are those yet to be found by science and, when discovered, these become not the possession of an elite but open to all. In secret societies, the notion of the big secret is a carrot on a stick – a psychological device to maintain loyalty and subservience. In the wider society, the idea that groups like the Knights Templar possess a grand secret has more to do with our expectations and our desire for mystery than it does with the reality of the organisation in question? Where there is mystery and the unknown, our urge is to fill the gaps with any number of false assumptions.

Another criticism of secret societies, more significant than that they pretend to hidden knowledge they don't have, is that they work beyond the law. At its simplest this is exemplified by the often-told tale of the policeman who stops a speeding car only to find the man behind the wheel is a fellow lodge member. With a quick wink he tells the driver to be on his way. (Would this not be true of two ordinary, non-secret society friends in a similar situation?) More importantly, it is often argued that the Skull and Bones society grooms future US leaders and that, through them, it exercises global power. But that says more about power and money than it does about the machinations of a secret society. Money is more powerful than any oath. Are the oil-hungry men of power manipulating the population for the good of their secret society or for the sake of their mutual bank balances? The latter is the most likely. All allegiances to secret oaths go out the window when Mammon beckons. As Milton wrote in *Paradise Lost*, 'his looks and thoughts were always downward bent, admiring more the riches of heaven's pavement, trodden gold, than aught divine or holy …'

It is more likely that the success of secret societies is down to fear – a deep motivating force for every human being. In a rapidly fracturing culture, where uncertainty is the order of the day, where the old orders are struggling to survive in the face of global, economic and natural pressures beyond their control, it is a tempting idea that some form of stability rests with a secret cadre who (apparently) have their finger on what is real. In the often harsh and brutal reality of modern culture, the isolated individual may seek solace in a higher power or the special knowledge of a secret society. A shared set of ideals allows an individual to feel part of a group which readily accepts him into their 'gang' as long as he plays by the rules – the rules that are needed to give that same individual boundaries. Real freedom is beyond the desire or capabilities of most and, in a society where rules may have disappeared or simply changed beyond comprehension, a secret society may offer the very things they are seeking – guidance, group think, common beliefs and community and, at the very least, companionship.

This book outlines the best-known secret societies, many of which still thrive today, although they have changed much in the years since they were created. As well as highlighting the various organisations themselves, paying particular attention to their beginnings and their power base, the book will attempt to explain why secret societies are so prolific and what the psychology behind them is. Why are they predominantly male? What is it about these clandestine groups that makes them so appealing? Why do so many insist that would-be members go through demeaning and peculiar initiation ceremonies? What real power do they wield in the modern world? Do they really affect the policies of governments? In short, do they really run the world, as conspiracy theorists would have us believe? As children we had dens and gangs; in adulthood we have lodges and secret societies.

Common to all secret societies:

They claim secret knowledge

They claim to be the 'true' keepers of that secret knowledge

They claim that the secret knowledge is the one paramount truth

They claim a long lineage – sometimes into ancient history – but in all cases these claims are unfounded

They are often persecuted by non-members – usually the church, which fears 'ungodly ways'

They are accused of having a hidden agenda to undermine society

They are elitist

They include ceremonies of ritualistic death – passing from the old life to the new – in their initiation rites

They swear oaths of allegiance / have secret handshakes or recognition methods

They threaten individual members with dire consequences if secrets are revealed

They often involve a charismatic leader or figurehead who claims to be the 'messiah' or a reincarnation of one

They are often the subject of conspiracy theories

They often play on their perceived power to induce fear and a degree of awe in the wider society

They do not possess real secrets, other than those in their initiation rites and their methods of mutual recognition

The Secret Societies

'I know that's a secret
For it is whispered everywhere ...'
William Congreve

Author's Note

Limitations of space mean that it is impossible to include all secret societies that have existed but the following are some of the best known. Organisations such as the *SS* and the *Tontons Macoute* have been omitted because, although they shared certain characteristics of secret societies, they were primarily secret police.

The Assassins

The Assassins were the fanatical branch of a secret Moslem sect called the Ismailis, whose esoteric teachings taught that all actions were morally ambivalent, and thus the Assassins were free to behave as they did. The word 'assassins', of course, has entered the English language to mean those prepared to kill for religious or political purposes. At their height the Assassins were the most feared secret organisation anywhere. An Assassin might lie in wait for years before striking at his intended target, often befriending the victim well before the deed was done. They inspired widespread terror because they seemed to have eyes and ears everywhere and were utterly ruthless in their methods.

They were founded around the middle of the 11th century by Hassan-ibn-Sabbah, a Shi'ite Moslem from Khorassan. He had studied Ismaili doctrine at Nishapur and from the religious leaders there he had gained a good understanding of their secret knowledge and reached one of highest levels within their organisation. But while in Cairo he argued furiously with the Ismaili leaders and was forced to leave Egypt and to head to Persia via Aleppo and Damascus. Once there he gathered followers around him and proceeded to take the rock-fortress of Alamut in 1090. It was here that he founded a sect not unlike the Ismailis, which adopted much of their teachings but had the added dimension of employing assassination techniques against all enemies.

At the head of this new order was the absolute ruler *Sheik-al-jebal* or the Old Man of the Mountains. Beneath him were three *Dai-al-kirbal* or grand priors, then the *Dais* or priors. At the fourth level were the *Refiks* who were associates with partial knowledge of certain aspects of the cult and, beneath them, were the *Fedavis* or *Fedais* (the devoted), the great uninitiated who were nonetheless devoted to the cause and blindly followed the orders of the Old Man of the Mountains. Before the Fedavis were sent on their assassination missions they were thrown into states of ecstasy and intoxication by the ingestion of hashish (hemp). From this act they were known as the *Hashishin* or hemp-eaters, a name that was subsequently changed to Assassin by western tongues. The *Lasiks* or novices, the sixth level of the order, and the labourers and mechanics, the seventh, had to follow the teachings of the Koran with the strictest observance. The initiated, in contrast, were given much greater freedom in religion and often considered religious teachings to be of little importance.

Hassan died in 1124 and his chief *dai*, Kia-Busurg-Omid took over. Under him the Assassins established themselves in Syria and soon proved their powerful position by murdering two Khalifs. In 1163 Hassan II set out to abolish Islam in the Assassin state. In its place he tried to open up the order to outsiders, passing on all secret knowledge to those outside the realm of the initiated. In keeping with Assassin traditions, he was murdered by his brother-in-law. His son, Mohammed II, who ruled with a rod of iron, entered into abortive negotiations with the Crusaders. Trying to unify the forces of Islam, Mohammed came up against Saladin and tried to have the Saracen leader killed by sending three Assassins to attack him. Unsurprisingly, this made the Assassins Saladin's enemy number one. In 1176, in an attempt to destroy the cult once and for all, Saladin invaded their territory and began to decimate it. Fearing total annihilation, the Assassins negotiated a truce with Saladin and ceased their attempts to kill him.

By this time two leaders were really running the Assassins, Hasan in Persia and Sinan in Syria. Sinan was a ruthless man who had decided that he was god incarnate. For most of the daylight hours he stood on an outcrop of rock, dressed only in a hair shirt, preaching his fire-and-brimstone belief in his own terrible power.

When Mohammed II died Jalaludin, his son, revoked Hasan's orders that the Assassins were to have no obvious religious observances and, realising that they could be more powerful with an outward appearance of piety, insisted on devotion to Islam. Cursing his predecessors for their actions, he convinced the powers of Islam of his sincerity and they made him a prince. Jalaludin was succeeded by the weak and ineffective Aladdin, a man who preferred tending his sheep to involving himself with the activities of the order. This was the beginning of the end for the Assassins who, at the same time, had to deal with the Mongol hordes sweeping in from the East.

Rukneddin, Aladdin's son, attempted to stem the Mongol tide but he was kidnapped and murdered. As a result the Assassins' power in Persia was destroyed and only a few stray members of the order were left to go underground and await a possible revival. In 1260 the Mamluk Sultan of Egypt repelled the Mongol armies and, in doing so, restored the fortress of Alamut – the former Assassin stronghold – and other possessions to the once-powerful order. Under Egyptian control the Assassins, now known as the 'Arrows of the Sultan of Egypt with which he reaches his enemies' had an upturn in their fortunes.

The Assassins remained a potent force throughout the Middle East for centuries and, although not as mighty as they once were, they continued to be a power in Islamic lands. They could even be found as far away as Bombay. The Assassins had immeasurable influence on other secret societies, starting with the Templars who took their system of grand masters, grand priors and their degrees of initiation from them. All Western secret societies which derive their basic structure and tenets from the Templars owe much to this ruthless order of devoted Ismailis.

The Bilderberg Group

'If the Bilderberg Group is not a conspiracy of some sort, it is conducted in such a way as to give a remarkably good imitation of one.'

C. Gordon Tether
The Financial Times 1975

Despite the accusations, the Bilderberg Group is not strictly a secret society but they do operate behind closed doors and spark much theory and controversy. It is included here because of its supposed links to the likes of the Illuminati, Freemasonry and the Bohemian Grove. There are no initiation ceremonies as such but the Group requires that its members have great experience in the areas in which they work – usually commerce, politics and banking. Like most groups that operate beyond the public eye, they are the target of bitter criticism, mostly from the Christian right who maintain that the group is part of a Jewish-Communist or Liberal-Zionist conspiracy to run the world. Of course there is also criticism from the far left who consider the Bilderberg Group to be nothing more than a right wing capitalist organisation bent on forming a one world government in conjunction with its cousin the Trilateral Commission. In a sense one can sympathise with the Bilderberg's desire to remain discreetly behind closed doors.

Unlike most secret societies the Bilderberg do have a genuine claim to be interested in world affairs — whatever power they have or are perceived to work under. It is true that many powerful men have been invited to join them but with individuals as different as Denis Healey, Jimmy Carter, Henry Kissinger, Kenneth Clark and George Bush senior involved it is hard to place the Bilderberg in the political spectrum. Powerful figures of both the left and right seem to co-exist happily together. Despite this apparently benign, all-encompassing stance there are those who feel that the Bilderberg represent a threat. In Yugoslavia, for example, leading Serbs have blamed Bilderberg for starting the war, which led to the downfall of Slobodan Milosevic. The Oklahoma City bomber Timothy McVeigh, the London nail-bomber David Copeland and Osama Bin Laden are all said to believe that the Bilderberg is behind the policies of all western governments. Evidence that a misplaced paranoid belief can have bloody consequences.

It has not helped matters that Will Hutton, the British economist and one-time Bilderberg delegate, has likened it to the annual WEF gathering where 'the consensus established is the backdrop against which policy is made world-wide.' Do the Bilderberg really run the show? Denis Healey, former Foreign Secretary and Labour peer was one of the original four who set up the group in 1954. His response to the accusation, from whichever political direction, that Bilderberg control the world's governments is usually a terse expletive. 'There's absolutely nothing in it. We never sought to reach a consensus on the big issues at Bilderberg. It's simply a place for discussion,' he says, adding that, 'Bilderberg is the most useful international group I ever attended. The confidentiality enabled people to speak honestly without fear of repercussions.' So what is the truth? So what is the Bilderberg Group?

The first meeting of the Bilderberg Group took place between 29 and 31 May 1954 at the Hotel de Bilderberg in the Dutch town of Oosterbeek and was one of the results of the spirit of post-war trans-Atlantic co-operation. The principal idea expressed was that future wars could be prevented by bringing world power-brokers together in an informal friendly setting away from inquisitive eyes, with assistance from the Dutch government and the CIA. The latter were presumably there as security but the presence of US Intelligence at this prestigious gathering of the world's top bankers, industrialists and politicians fuelled much of the conspiratorial theorising about the set-up that has followed. It is no surprise to Alasdair Spark, an expert in conspiracy theories, that activists have seized on Bilderberg. 'The idea that a shadowy clique is running the world is nothing new. For hundreds of years people have believed the world is governed by a cabal of Jews.' He adds, 'Shouldn't we expect that the rich and powerful organise things in their own interests? It's called capitalism.'

While those on the far right and some libertarians accuse Bilderberg of being a 'liberal Zionist plot', leftists such as activist Tony Gosling, a former journalist, are also vocal in their criticism. Gosling states: 'My main problem is the secrecy. When so many people with so much power get together in one place I think we are owed an explanation of what is going on.' And he adds: 'One of the first places I heard about the determination of US forces to attack Iraq was from leaks that came out of the 2002 Bilderberg meeting.'

In Bilderberg's defence Martin Wolf, a reporter for the

Financial Times says, 'It's privacy, rather than secrecy, that is key to such a meeting. The idea that such meetings cannot be held in private is fundamentally totalitarian,' he says. 'It's not an executive body; no decisions are taken there.'

Once a year the world's most powerful people meet in a heavily guarded location, usually a hotel. These conferences have taken place in such diverse places as Hot Springs, Virginia, Torquay in the United Kingdom, Cannes in France and Fredensborg in Denmark. A while before the meeting is due to take place security teams, generally the CIA, move in and prepare the ground, emptying the venue of any guests. The involvement of the CIA has its roots in the work of one Doctor Joseph Hieronim Retinger, a Pole who lived a chequered and varied life, in which he went from abject poverty to a position in which he had the ear of the President of the United States.

Retinger, one of the most mysterious characters of the twentieth century, has been declared the father of the Bilderberg group. It was rumoured that he had been an agent for Socialiste Internationale, the Freemasons, the Vatican and the Mexican government. But his employment also took in such vocations as reading to the staff of a Cuban cigar factory and forming a secret society made up of young Mexican patriots called the Action Committee. In 1924 the idea of a united Europe first occurred to him and he decided, with the help of British Member of Parliament E. D. Morel, to form a clandestine group whose sole purpose was to encourage such an endeavour. When Morel died, Retinger talked with politicians like Ernest Bevin and Sir Stafford Cripps but neither was particularly impressed with his ideas and the project stalled on the outbreak of the Second World War.

After spending time with the Polish Government in Exile

in London with General Sikorski and the SOE under Sir Colin Gubbins, Retinger returned to the idea again and, in 1946, he made a speech to the Royal Institute for International Affairs which emphasised the potential threat from Soviet Russia. Two years later, knowing that they would need the support of the United States, former Belgian Prime Minister Paul Spaak, Winston Churchill and Duncan Sandys, President of the European Movement, an organisation born out of the speech made two years earlier, accompanied Retinger on a finance-raising mission. While in the United States the American Committee on a United Europe (ACUE) was launched under the supervision of William Donovan, former director of the OSS (Office of Strategic Services) with Allen Dulles as Vice - Chairman. Dulles had recently been made director of the newly created CIA. Money was soon forthcoming and to-talled nearly half a million pounds in the first four years.

Retinger then decided that unofficial meetings should take place between important people from NATO countries and, through one of his European Movement colleagues Paul Rijkens, he made an important contact in Prince Bernhard of the Netherlands, a man chosen to be an ideal figurehead to help promote European unity and to spearhead an Atlantic alliance. At this time there was a rising tide of anti-Americanism and Retinger felt this was not a positive development so he rounded up a number of important people from countries including Denmark, Greece, Italy, France and the UK and held the first meeting in a Paris apartment on 25 September 1952. It was agreed that, if they were to expand their ideals, the United States had to be a key player so Retinger and Prince Bernhard once more went to Washington to state their case.

In the US they garnered the support of General Walter

Bedell Smith, director of the CIA and Charles Jackson, President Eisenhower's national security assistant. The result of a successful meeting was the setting up of an American Committee, the membership of which included David Rockefeller of Chase Manhattan Bank and Henry Heinz of the famous food manufacturer. The first formal meeting then took place at the Hotel de Bilderberg.

Since that time the list of names of those who have attended the meetings of this illustrious organisation has included Henry Kissinger, Cyrus Vance, ex-President Gerald Ford, Sir Keith Joseph, Sir David Owen, Vice President Walter Mondale, Valerie Giscard d'Estaing, Helmut Schmidt and every British Prime Minister over the last forty years. One commentator, the media guru Marshall McLuhan, found the whole thing dull and uninspiring and 'nearly suffocated at the banality and irrelevance.' But it is clear that large numbers of people with influence in the media, politics, economics and corporate business have been invited to attend a Bilderberg meeting at some time.

Despite the denials of those involved it is interesting to note that a number of important world events were born within Bilderberg gatherings. The Treaty of Rome, which created the Common Market, and both Gulf wars had their genesis within this secretive organisation and the French complained that the Bilderberg had interfered with the politics of France's government in the 1960s. No doubt numerous other domestic and foreign policies for member countries, both large and small-scale, had their roots within the machinations of this group but, as records of meetings are banned from being published, the true extent of its global influence is unclear.

It may very well be that the Bilderberg has everyone's best interests at heart and that the conspiracy theories which surround it are, at the least, naive. But the fact remains that they are there to shape public opinion and to steer certain world events as they see fit. Robert Eringer, in his book *The Global Manipulators*, is happy to have world leaders meet behind closed doors but, as a caveat, he asks what is it that is being said that demands this level of secrecy. When world leaders speak of the spread of democracy, why do these same people then commit to operating behind closed doors in a media blackout?

The Bohemian Grove

The activities of the Bohemian Grove provide a contrast to the apparent seriousness of the Bilderberg Group but, like the Bilderberg, the Illuminati and others, they are supposed to be a group intent on global domination and a 'New World Order'. One conspiracy theorist, David Icke, is adamant that the Bohemian Grove is a front for the activities of giant anthropomorphic lizards who burn children in late-night rituals and worship the god Molech (the same one the Illuminati bow down before). This seems unlikely and is further evidence, if any were needed, that secret societies act as magnets for every foolish and daft notion in existence.

The Bohemian Club was started in San Francisco in 1872 and was founded by journalists and writers as an excuse for late-night social drinking. Its membership, in its early decades, included literary heavyweights like Jack London and Mark Twain. But the membership soon began to change. One member, Ed Bosque, decided to encourage a new input of members but to draw them from the very stratum of society that bohemians are most antagonistic towards – wealthy businessmen. As more and more wealthy men joined, the original Bohemians found themselves in the minority and, over the years, the rich replaced the poor. Oscar Wilde, on a visit to the Grovers, remarked that, 'I have never seen so many well-dressed, well-fed, businesslike looking bohemians in all my life.'

Tiring of their city meetings, the wealthy Bohemians decided to add a spiritual dimension to their proceedings. They would, they decided, commune with nature. They bought nearly three thousand acres of a giant Sequoia forest close to the Californian town of Monte Rio. By the time the new wealthy members took to the trees, the original Bohemians had lost control.

The Bohemian Grove rituals, mostly pseudo-druidic and created by a real-estate speculator called George Sterling who committed suicide in 1926, begin on 14 July with a ceremony that banishes 'Care'. An effigy representing 'Care' is brought into a clearing surrounded by robed figures and mounted horsemen and is burnt. The flame of eternal friendship is then lit. Thus worldly worries are set aside and forgotten so the Grovers can begin their three weeks of carefree activities. They have a saying, 'Weaving spiders come not near,' which means that there is supposed to be no shop talk for the entire period of the gathering.

The Bohemians are split up into camps similar in structure to that of American fraternity houses and number one hundred and twenty in all. They sport names such as Hillbillies (to which George Bush Snr and Walter Cronkite belong), Owl's Nest (Ronald Reagan), Meyerling, Silverado Squatters, Totem Inn, Wayside Log, Ye Merrie Yowls and Zaca. Other famous members of the Bohemian Grove have included former Secretary of State George Schultz, Leonard Firestone, Gerald Ford, Richard Nixon, Henry Kissinger, James Baker, Herman Wouk, Charlton Heston, Teddy Roosevelt, Herbert Hoover, Dick Cheney and Edward Teller.

Membership is largely for Americans only and it takes years for a newcomer to be admitted. Foreign visitors are, however, often invited to address the US elite and perhaps entertain themselves with a few games of dominoes – apparently the game of choice in the Bohemian Grove. They can also listen to lectures about world economics and science or watch the elaborate, lowbrow stage plays, bristling with double entendres, which are planned five years in advance.

Other more licentious activities are also said to take place which involve the heavy use of alcohol, drugs of various forms (including one that maintains five-hour erections), the hiring of prostitutes and gay sex. A whole service industry has built up around the Bohemian Grove which caters for the excesses of the membership and which makes it welcome, for economic reasons, in that part of California. Big money is being made off 'Big Money'. In contrast, the Bohemian Grove Action Network works to bring about the downfall of the activities of the Grovers. In the last decade, the conspiracy theories suggesting the place is a site of a 'secret government' have been less widespread, although rumours still persist. The critics still need an enemy to maintain their own survival. The most likely explanation of the Bohemian Grove is that it is just a glorified frat house for those who miss their days at university in which men of power can act irresponsibly and let off steam.

The Castrators of Russia

All secret societies have initiation ceremonies in which rites are performed and the passing from an old world, that of the profane, to an enlightened one, that of the order, is represented. But no initiation ceremony can be as extreme as that employed by the Castrators of Russia. Also known as the 'Skoptsi' (i.e. 'Castrated'), their influence spread far and wide and, despite the severe nature of their initiation process, they made many thousands of converts, from the humblest citizen to the aristocracy of Russia and the Balkans. Many considered them to be mad (it is not hard to understand why) but the insane among their ranks were very much in the minority.

The Skoptsi beliefs were focused on a version of Christianity but their ideas were really based in the old mystery schools in which saints, monks and ascetics could attain an affinity with the divine by removing the baser instincts of sexual temptation. Even in certain pagan cults, castration was an acceptable way to celebrate devotion to, for example, the mother goddess. The intention was to suppress the libido and drive that potent sexual energy into religious fervour.

They were born out of the Sect of Flagellants in around 1757, whose most famous later adherent was Rasputin. The Russian government did not hear of the Skoptsi's existence until 1771 by which time self-inflicted wounding, as part of a religious rite, had reached almost epidemic level. The whole purpose of the Flagellants' ceremony or 'Radenyi' was to reach a religious ecstasy. To achieve this they used a combination of Christian and pagan rituals, with invocations and hymns producing a whirling rhythm, while the participants danced themselves into a state of trance. Anyone who saw fit to grow tired suffered the vigorous lashings of the master of ceremonies who whipped him or her back into step. The rituals always ended in an orgy of convulsive fits and ecstatic states.

The authorities moved to quash these activities and, in one incident, arrested a man called Andrei Ivanov and swiftly tried and convicted him for persuading thirteen fellow peasants to ritually castrate themselves during such orgiastic pursuits. He was ably assisted by Kondratji Selivanov, a man from Stolbovo in the Province of Orel. During the trial in St Petersburg there was widespread puzzlement at such activities, as no one could believe that anyone would genuinely want to castrate himself in order to become part of some oddly masochistic secret society. However, the Skoptsi believed that a great secret would only be confided to the adherent once he had made that sacrifice.

Although Ivanov was sentenced to spend the rest of his days in Siberia, Selivanov fled to Tambov where he started to preach his doctrine that religious fulfilment and salvation lay in the supreme sacrifice – what he euphemistically called the 'Baptism of Fire'. The ritual was usually performed using a red hot poker, but knives, hatchets, shards of glass and razors were also employed. This was something the cult claimed that Christ and the early Christians practised. Within a short period he had gained a fervent disciple, Alexander Ivanov Shilov, and had made numerous converts to his belief system who met regularly for frenzied activity in which they encouraged each other towards castration. Selivanov, now quite plump and bald, allegedly as a result of his own castration, moved to Moscow to broaden his doctrinal horizons but there his attempts to avoid the authorities failed. He was swiftly arrested and sent to Siberia while several followers were beaten mercilessly. Others who had not submitted themselves to castration were told to keep quiet and to avoid active recruitment but, despite the capture and internment of the prime mover of the castration cult, the movement continued to grow. The authorities remained baffled by this expansion.

Selivanov escaped and made his way once more to Moscow where the Tsar first gave him an audience and then promptly sent him to an asylum. On the accession of the mystically orientated Alexander I, who was dominated by a religious aristocrat, Baroness Krudner, Selivanov was released. The Baroness considered the interned man as nothing short of a saint and, within a short time, had introduced him to the high and mighty of Russia. Many fell under Selivanov's spell. Among these new recruits was Alexei Jelanski a State Councillor and an extremely powerful man, powerful enough to keep the authorities away from the Skoptsi. Jelanski too was initiated into the cult, enduring the 'Baptism of Fire', and eventually he became a castrator himself.

It was not long before Selivanov was set up in a large house, known as the House of God, New Jerusalem or Heavenly Zion, the upkeep of which was maintained by his disciples who continued to seek out new recruits, particularly in the ranks of the influential. Here the ceremonies continued unabated, rituals that the Skoptsi believed would bring them great joy in life. Selivanov maintained he was a reincarnation of Christ, who, according to his doctrine, was himself the physical manifestation of an earlier unnamed deity. It was also around this time that the Tsarina gave up her stately position and, under an assumed name, dedicated her life completely to the cult. Having stayed for a while in the house of a Skoptsi prophet, she retired to a sanctuary where it was said she could transfer divine powers to visiting adherents.

Selivanov himself began to propagate myths about his background, a not uncommon practice among gurus and self-promoted cult leaders throughout history. He claimed that, as soon as he reached adulthood, he castrated himself and convinced others that this emasculating process was the only way to reach salvation. His story was backed up by the apparent miracles he performed as a direct result, he said, of his sacrifice. At this point his claims became more overblown and incredible although such was the power that Selivanov had over his doting acolytes that they continued to be believed.

Selivanov claimed that he inherited the throne under the name of Peter III and was forced to marry Catherine II who rapidly decided that her new husband, not being a complete man, was not for her and decided that he must be assassinated. Forewarned of this, the 'Tsar' fled, swapping identities with a soldier who met the fate planned for a speedily retreating Peter III. Once free, the man who had ruled Russia took on the mantle of a peasant and changed his name to Selivanov. His popularity with the members of the aristocracy, who later flocked to join the cult, was proof enough for his followers that he had indeed once been of a privileged status. To further back up his messiah status it was claimed that Shilov, his first disciple, was the announcer of the coming Redeemer, John the Baptist to Selivanov's Christ.

Selivanov, as all prophets eventually do, wrote a promotional book entitled *The Book of the Passion of (Selivanov) The Redeemer*. In this book he claimed that Tsar Paul I had brought the Redeemer back to Moscow to hand him the crown because he knew the real identity of the exiled mystic – that he was the earlier Tsar. Because Selivanov demanded that Paul be castrated in order to become a true believer in the one true faith, the Tsar had imprisoned him in an asylum. With his manhood threatened, the ruling Tsar locked 'his father' away from public view.

When Alexander I came to the throne, it is claimed he joined Selivanov's sect and his wife joined shortly afterwards. The real threat to the prophet then came from members of the Tsar's government who felt he had undue influence over the rulers of the country and moved to confine him once more. After he was locked up in the monastery of Suzdal, Selivanov made the bold statement that he would live forever and that he would eventually return to rule Russia, at which point everyone would become Skoptsi. This belief prevailed long after his death and even existed up to recent times. (Although more recently followers of the precepts altered the rules, allowing two children before the act of castration was performed.)

Even after Selivanov's death in 1832 Skoptsism proved a durable faith. It continued to spread across Russia and into all walks of life despite persecution of the society after the accession of Tsar Nicholas I. Many adherents were sent to Siberia but nothing seemed able to stop the cult or curb the continuing enthusiasm for its doctrines. Despite considerable efforts by the authorities, people continued to mutilate themselves for their faith. The cult's survival was due, in part, to the fact that the Skoptsi, especially in the twentieth century, donated large sums of money to churches, priests and officials. Much of this money may have been nothing more than bribes or intended to keep the wrong people from asking the right questions but the Skoptsi came to be considered great benefactors.

What is still puzzling is why emasculation was (and sometimes still is) so popular. Self-mutilation is considered to be a step to mystical knowledge and is as old as religion itself. Perhaps there is something Freudian to it. It is a self-destructive urge related to the death wish (see *Man Against Himself* by Dr K. Menninger). In weak-minded people, under the influence of skilled mind-manipulators, the sense of self preservation can be subjugated. However, this does not fully explain how the Skoptsi, whose converts were from all walks of life and all levels of society and cannot all have been intrinsically weak-willed, could persuade so many to undertake the Baptism of Fire.

The Cathars

The Cathars (taken from the Greek word for 'pure') were a sect of the Middle Ages, owing something to the ideas of Gnosticism. Catharism is supposed to have developed among the Slavs in Southern Macedonia and, from there, spread over southern and western Europe. In Thrace there was a similar sect, who had been transported there, called the Paulicians, later known as the Bogomils. In the second half of the 12th century they were strongest in Albania and Slovenia and were divided into two branches, the Albanensians (the extremists) and the Concorezensians (named after Goriza in Albania). In Italy the heresy appeared in Turin around 1035 and remained active until the 14th century. There its adherents were known as Patarini, named after the *Pataria*, a street in Milan where they held their secret meetings in 1058.

The Cathars reached their greatest strength in Southern France where they more commonly known as Albigenses or Poblicants, a corruption of the word Paulicians. After the great Albigensian war the Inquisition systematically rooted them out and, after the early 14th century, they disappeared from history. The only Cathar document that has survived is a short ritual written in the Romance language of the Troubadours.

They based their teachings on the New Testament and the

apocryphal *Vision of Isaiah* and the *Gospel of John*. They held for the most part, Manichean views of the world. (Manicheans were followers of a prophet called Mani who taught that the universe was controlled by the two antagonistic powers of good and evil – an old Babylonian nature worship that was modified by Persian and Christian influences.) The Cathars practised a rigid asceticism and believed that deliverance from evil was only achieved by turning away from the material world. They renounced marriage and possessions and followed a strict vegetarian diet. They were separated into the 'Believers' or the *Credentes* and the *Perfecti* who had received the 'laying on of hands'. Baptism of the Spirit was called the *Consolamentum*. In 1240 these 'pure ones', numbering some 4000, formed the Catharist Church, in their words 'the only true and pure church on earth'.

The Charcoal Burners

The Charcoal Burners or *Carbonari* of Italy are one of the few secret societies with an overt political agenda. In the early part of the 19th century they were a strong force that had related groups in Germany, Poland and France. Although an Italian secret society, they claim that their roots are in Scotland. Or so the myth goes.

King Francis of France met the original Carbonari who, at that time, it is said, were a group of mystics. Francis had strayed across the border of his kingdom and had encountered the group who were hiding out in the wilderness after escaping tyrannical repression. They avoided suspicion by working as burners of charcoal, which they then sold in various towns and villages where they met their supporters. They used signs, words and touches to help in mutual recognition. With no houses in the forests they built square lodges or *vendite*, three in number, in which their government sat. These lodges were divided into *barracas* with each being run by a *Gran Maestro* or grand master. King Francis was promptly initiated in the order and took up the role of grand protector of the Carbonari in his native France.

The Carbonari promptly spread through France, Germany and England where it became known as 'Forest Masonry'. They practised their own religions free from the interference of the Catholic Church. They struck up alliances with other secret societies, most successfully with the Freemasons. Members were called 'Good Cousins' and were divided into Apprentices and Masters. They were supposed to be engaged in good works and protection of the needy and the most important of their basic tenets was humility. Their objectives included gathering together enough like-minded men for any action required against repression by the government or the military. In one Carbonari document it states that the only way for the average man to gain any justice and welfare is to form a secret society against the selfish redoubt of those in power.

The Carbonari claim that their ancestry can be traced back to ancient mysteries including the cult of Mithra, the Gnostics and the Templars but more likely their antecedents were the semi-political groups of 12th century Southern Italy. These included the *Avengers* of 1186, a kind of Mafia precursor, and the *Beati Paoli* who dedicated themselves to destroying corrupt power bases. The Beati Paoli were especially ruthless, employing all kinds of brutal methods to further their aims, and it is said that they are still in existence. It was from them that the Carbonari took the practice of cursing defecting members and the idea that the names of defectors would be included in a 'black book'.

Despite the more brutal aspects of the order, individual initiates were expected to show generosity and kindness towards those of a lower status. The Carbonari were expected to show benevolence and justice when required. They were not allowed to consort with the mistresses or the wives of fellow Cousins and had to live lives of exemplary morality. There were penalties for those who disobeyed the basic laws, the very least of which was that the wayward Cousin would have his name written into the black book.

In the early 19th century the Carbonari were revolutionaries and led uprisings against the old order in Naples, Piedmont and elsewhere, working towards the eventual unification of Italy. In the 1820s the order was run out of Italy and found exile in France but, later in the century, when the efforts of famous Italian patriots like Garibaldi, Mazzini and Cavour had resulted in a united Italy, it was allowed to return.

The Cult of Abramelin

Abramelin was a mage and supposed creator of a powerful manuscript that resides in the Bibliothéque de L'Arsenal in Paris. The cult is a complete magical training system that the acolyte learns through dedication, practice and the use of certain diagrams that are so powerful that they are not allowed to be shown to anyone outside of the cult. Eliphas Levi and Aleister Crowley were adherents. The book, according to many, is the ultimate book of its kind.

Once more there are claims for great provenance for the work which was apparently translated from the original Hebrew into French in 1458. The work is Jewish in origin and is said to contain the sacred magic given by God to Moses, David and Solomon. Once more, levels of initiation are undertaken with a variety of purification rituals and the use of a young child, between the ages of six and eight, who acts as a medium between the magician and the Guardian Angel who watches over the works of the follower of the secret cult.

The manuscript itself is in fact three books of 413 pages and, as well as magical rites, contains an autobiographical text by Abraham the Jew along with Cabbalistic diagrams. Variations of the cult appear in India and Persia. The one major difference between the Cult of Abramelin and the standard secret society structure is that the follower is self-initiated and has no spiritual mentor until the final experience of contact with the Guardian Angel.

The Cult of the Black Mother

This is a predominantly Indian phenomenon and is part of the Thugee tradition. The Thugs believed that Bhowani or 'Kali the Black One' bestowed success on the worthy but demanded the sacrifice of lives in return. It is based on a myth that was taught to every young Thug that Kali, born of Shiva, represents the evil spirit, delighting in human blood, presiding over plague, pestilence, storms and all that brings ill to humanity.

The Cult of Mithra

'*The Mithraic Rites have been maintained by a constant tradition, with their penances and tests of the courage of the candidate for admission, through the Secret Societies of the Middle Ages and the Rosicrucians, down to the modern faint reflex of the latter, the Freemasons ...*'

Knight *Symbolic Language*

Mithra or Mithras was the ancient Persians' god of light, one of their chief deities, and Mithraism is one of the few cults than can claim a genuine heritage of at least six thousand years. Mithra was considered ruler of the universe but was often a synonym for the sun. The direct translation of Mithra is 'friend' and he was so called because he befriended man in life and then protected him from evil after death. His image was that of a young man wearing a Phrygian cap, a tunic and a mantle over his left shoulder and plunging a sword into the neck of a fearsome bull. He was the direct link between the affairs of men and the great deity of Ormuzd. Initially he was seen as a genie, one of twenty-eight, but he soon grew in stature to become the only one that had any major significance for his followers. He was also the first lesser representative of a deity to surpass the higher power in significance.

From its Persian origins, Mithraism spread to Babylonia, to

Greece and then finally to the Roman Empire where it came into conflict with the early cult of Christianity. Despite losing out to the new faith it blossomed in various corners of the declining Empire. Evidence of its spread can be found even in London (Temple Court, 11 Queen Victoria Street) and Housesteads in Northumberland where it was a favourite with the legions. The famous chapel at Rosslyn – related, it sometimes seems, to every secret society in existence – is also built on the site of a former Temple of Mithra. Further archaeological evidence is paltry at best but a great deal of secret knowledge continued to thrive in the East, particularly in Syria and India, and much survived by later being absorbed into other secret societies. One of the best ways to give a new society more gravitas is to claim a great lineage through words, phrases and a history which are grafted on from the ideas it has 'borrowed' from another cult.

The Mithraists had three ritualistic and sacred objects. These were the *Bull*, which (as it often does) stood for virility, nature, strength and growth, the *Hammer* (sometimes a club), which represented man's creativity, and the *Crown*, which represented the sun and supernatural power. They believed that by learning what the symbols meant and what they represented man could rid himself of the world and become successful at all he undertook. The ultimate reward was that of a happy afterlife.

Whereas Christianity was open to all (or, at least, the majority of the population), Mithraism had an elitist attitude and only those considered worthy could become adherents. This elitism contributed to Mithraism's decline. Christianity thrived but, as Christianity has always done, it adopted much that the other faith had to offer, most notably the emotive ritualistic side of Mithraism. Modern Christians are mostly unaware that some of what they hold dear derives from the Persians and their worship of the sun.

In Mithraism the Sacrament was the first level of initiation. It also went under the name of the Crow and was open to any acolyte who could keep a secret and seemed interested in developing his knowledge of the cult and becoming a full-time worshipper. It was the 'baptism' stage in which the old life and its inherent shackles, together with any previous belief systems, were cast off and the new life of Mithraism was adopted. The parallels with the Gnostic idea of 'resurrection' within a lifetime, not after it, are clear. The initiate 'died' ritualistically and was 'reborn' as a new man, above and beyond the rest of uninitiated humanity.

The symbolic use of the word 'Crow' stems, in all likelihood, from the Persian ceremony of exposing the dead to carrion birds, something still performed by the *Parsi* in India whose beliefs have come in part from the Iranian *Zoroaster*.

The ritual itself took place within an underground temple constructed to look like a natural cavern (symbolic of death) where the aspirant had to perform tests of initiation. These took the form of a pursuit by priests dressed in animal skins and culminated in a three-day fast in which the exhausted newcomer was 'brainwashed' into surrendering all ties with the family. From that point on, nothing mattered more than the worship of Mithra. The newly 'reborn' initiate was then shown, amid a cacophony of drums and cymbals, a great statue of Mithra holding a bull by its hind legs. As in so many cults and religions the basic idea was to overcome the sexual urge so that libidinous energy could be channelled away from the baser drives towards a more spiritual realm. The bull, representing those passionate sexual urges, was seen to be in a state of supplication. It was literally 'held' in check – conquered and defeated so that the enlightened soul could work towards higher matters. The Mithraists followed a path that many secret societies, as well as a multitude of cults and religions do – one in which disciplined 'power' is produced through a harsh management of the sexual urge.

After the noisy procession to the statue of the bull came 'communion' with the higher powers through the drinking of wine, from a holy cymbal, and the eating of bread from a drum (the two instruments used to create the music). The bread eaten by the initiate represented Mithra and, by doing so, he was ready to accept the sun god as the source of all nourishment. (The parallels with Christianity are more than coincidental. As already stated, Christianity took much from Mithraism.) At this point the secret password was given to him thus enabling him to identify with the cult and be identified by other members of the cult. Again this is something common to all secret societies.

The second level of initiation was called 'The Secret' and in this ceremony the candidate, disorientated and in a state of induced 'ecstasy', was made to believe that the great statue of Mithra had come to life. No archaeological evidence has been found for the use of any mechanical method in this so the whole thing must have been the product of an altered consciousness. The initiate was brought before the statue and made an offering of bread and water to show his subservience to Mithra, swearing an oath to this effect and becoming, in a sense, a 'soldier' of Mithra. (This aspect of Mithraism contributed to its popularity with the majority of ranks within the Roman army as the cult was spread to all corners of the empire.)

A sun sign or cross was then made on the forehead of the initiate marking him as owned by Mithra. (Once more the parallels with Christianity are clear. The ritual of baptism and the mark of a cross being made on the forehead have links to this.) A crown was then held before him on the end of a sword which he would take and cast aside with the words, 'Mithra alone is my crown'. (It is worth noting that all crowns are derived from those of Persia, which were made in representation of the sun. Once more pagan ritualistic icons have survived happily within Christian contexts, their original meanings buried or deliberately forgotten.) More mock combat then followed and the candidate had to pit himself against man and beast, the trials again taking place within caves until he had symbolically slain all before him. As well as being a metaphor for death or the underworld, caves, of course, can represent the 'womb' from which the newly initiated member can be reborn. Many secret societies have the inner sanctum or the sanctum sanctorum – the holy of holies where the great secret is often kept and it is there that the resurrection rites are performed in which the rebirthing symbolism is at its most potent.

Should the followers of Mithra then decide that they had had enough of the outside world and want to dedicate themselves entirely to the god they would elect to go through the 'third degree' ceremony, that of the 'Lion', after which the initiates would become monks. Most of the Mithraic schools had seven degrees leading towards enlightenment but there were some variants offering as many as twelve. In the third the candidate would once more enter the subterranean world and have honey smeared across his brow. He was then given further training in the workings of Mithraism and further 'secrets' were revealed to him.

The Lion degree could only be undertaken during the period when the sun was in the zodiacal sign of Leo – in Persian the month was called *Asad*. Much astrological law could be found in Mithraism. In Greek versions of the cult, Mithras was given the spelling *Meitras* and, in the practice of numerology, this word was assigned the number 365 – tying in the god to the year and thus adding even more powerful symbolism.

Throughout the Roman period and beyond, the followers of Mithraism were held in high esteem, even garnering high praise from Christian writers who admonished fellow believers and advised them to take a leaf out of the book of the Mithraists and become better, more upright citizens. It was not in any sense an antisocial secret society – one criticism levelled at most others – because its aims did not conflict with the morals and ethics of the nation state in which it was developing. It did not threaten the power of the state so it was left alone. Eventually, over the centuries, its adherents became fewer and fewer and it all but disappeared – but that is not to say it became extinct. Other secret societies, the Rosicrucians and the Freemasons among them, have selected elements to include within their own ceremonies but it lives on most recognisably within Christianity, once its rival but now the vessel through which it survives. Mithraism's greatest ceremony was the Birth of the Sun which took place on 25 December – now a date of great importance to the followers of Christ.

The Decided Ones of Jupiter the Thunderer

This was an Italian cabal that came into existence in 1815 and was comprised of bandits, brigands and outlaws who were operating around Calabria and Abruzzi. It was set up by a notorious villain called Ciro Annunchiarico after the government decided to stamp out their activities. Annunchiarico, thug though he was, was also a learned man brought up in comfortable surroundings who drew on his education and upbringing to create his society. He was also head of another secret society, the *Patrioti Europi*. Lodges of the cabal were known as *Decisi* (Decisions) and the society was divided into 'Camps' of about three hundred men and 'Squadrons' of forty or so. Their aim was to make war against the 'tyrants of the universe' and each member had a document of membership part-written in blood.

The Freemasons

The Freemasons must be the most misunderstood of all secret societies. For centuries they have been the scapegoats for all kinds of miscreant activity and nefarious deeds. They have been despised by the Church, particularly Roman Catholicism, and Nazis alike and are still viewed with equal amounts of suspicion, fear, anger and hysterical paranoia by the general public, who see them as nothing more than an elitist and patriarchal club that flouts the law and behaves in a clandestine manner. Even as far back as 1797, Robison's *Proof of a Conspiracy* made furious accusations against the Freemasons, claiming that their symbolism concealed a dangerous conspiracy against government and religion. What is without doubt is that Freemasonry has supplied numerous other secret societies, both transient and longer lasting, with all kinds of rituals, rites and ceremonies.

Freemasonry claims a long heritage, dating back to the building of the Temple of Solomon, but this is extremely unlikely. Most scholars accept that its origins date to the medieval period when stone masons were in high demand for the building of the magnificent cathedrals of the time. In the *The Hiram Key,* Christopher Knight and Robert Lomas dispute this, claiming the origin of the Freemasons to be in ancient Egypt with the Pharaohs. Other writers maintain that

Freemasonry can be traced no further back than the 18th century when aristocratic gentlemen, with nothing better to do, formed an order, similar in many respects to the well-known Hell Fire Club, for private carousing. The Knights Templar and the Roman Empire are also claimed as the origin of the movement. The reality is that no one, not even the Freemasons themselves, is sure how far back the brotherhood goes.

Certainly the adjective 'free' as in Freemasons was originally used in the Middle Ages as an abbreviation for 'freeman masons' (i.e. those free of a guild). The Masonic brotherhoods of the middle ages were not too dissimilar to other guilds that existed at the time. They were governed by their own rules and regulations and drew on apprentices who had proved their worth. The masons were valued above all other guilds because of their skill with stone. Because of their vocation a great deal of travelling was required and masons lived a peripatetic life. It became desirable to develop methods of recognition for the fraternity so that, wherever he went, a mason could prove who he was and his level of competence. The idea that masons were in the possession of great secrets soon developed and that these great secrets enabled them to design the cathedrals. The truth was less dramatic. The only secrets the masons possessed concerned the correct way to dress and set stone and the architects, the real force behind church construction, were not members of the masonic fraternity. This is not to say the masons were just rude mechanicals. They were highly skilled men who could not only impart their own individuality into their carving but were aware of the works of their predecessors, profiting from their experiences and learning from the mistakes made. In 14th century Germany the masons did actually take on the role of architects, although it is claimed that the designs lack the 'higher' elements of non-masonic architects.

Modern Freemasonry, or 'speculative' Freemasonry as it is sometimes known, is an innocent mystification unconnected either with the building craft or architecture. It is English in origin and dates from the 18th century. It was founded for the 'practice of moral and social virtue' and was motivated by an overriding sense of charity and fraternal assistance. There are three main grades or degrees – Apprentice, Fellow-Craft and Master Mason. (There are also another thirty degrees above these main ones.) When the brother reaches Master Mason, all rights and privileges of the Lodge are granted to him. The Masons believe in the Grand Architect of the Universe, a conveniently flexible figure which can represent any 'Supreme Being' worshipped by any individual in the Brotherhood.

The lodges of Scotland claim to trace their origin to foreign masons in the 12th century who built the Abbeys of Melrose, Kilwinning and Holyrood. Those of England state that they originated with a group of masons who worked for King Athelstan in York around 926. Both lay claim to connections with Templars who settled in Britain after the demise of the order in mainland Europe. In 1717 a Grand Lodge was formed in London and, through this, charters for other lodges could be granted. It fell out of favour with the older York lodge because of its willingness to introduce innovations to the brotherhood and to grant charters to new lodges that were in the district which York claimed as its own. In 1813 the two lodges were brought together by their respective Grand Masters, the Dukes of Kent and Sussex and since then the Freemasons have been managed by the United Grand Lodge of Ancient Free and Accepted Masons of England. As well as granting charters the Grand Lodge is the acknowledged authority on in-house rules and regulations and acts as an arbitration body when internal disputes arise.

Modern Freemasonry spread from Britain worldwide and into such diverse locations as the United States and India. It was introduced to France in 1720, the US in 1730 – many famous Freemasons became involved in the later War and Declaration of Independence – Russia in 1740 and Germany in 1740. The United States of America may, in fact, have started as the ideal Masonic Republic since numerous Masons were party to the country's creation.

There is much written about the Freemasons and their activities. Some of the literature is moderately enlightened but there is much that is either nonsense or ludicrously off target. Much demonstrates only the ignorance of the writers. The Masons have been accused of bearing responsibility for everything from the Jack the Ripper murders to the World Trade Center attacks. Certainly there are those that will exploit Freemasonry for their own gain but to what extent is always open to speculation.

One accusation is that the Freemasons 'look after their own' and that promotion, particularly within such institutions as the police force or the military, is impossible without being a Freemason. But nepotism exists in all institutions and it seems unlikely that the Masons are guiltier of it than others. The Roman Catholic Church has been the source of many malevolent accusations against the Masons over the centuries, levelling charges of pantheism, devil worship and atheism at the lodges. It has even claimed that they are the instigators of all of the revolutions that have occurred in Europe. It has been condemned in papal bulls and encyclicals from seven popes, including Leo XIII and Pius X.

Any deep symbolic meaning hidden in the Freemasons' jargon is as apocryphal as the dangers they supposedly represent and their assumed desires to subvert governments and the law. The potential of the Freemasons has been ludicrously exaggerated. A set of passwords and secret handshakes do not make a New World Order. If anything, the Masons have, in the last two hundred years and more, attempted to develop tolerance and progressive thinking in many areas. Yet still, wherever there is a conspiracy theory, the Freemasons will appear somewhere in the mix. Usually it is as much a surprise to them as it is to anyone. They must be the busiest plotters of world domination that have ever existed. Certainly they are the most maligned of all secret societies.

The Garduna

The Garduna, or the Holy Warriors of Spain, claim to have been in existence for a long time, 1200 years, but it is more likely that the organisation has been around only since the fifteenth century. They also claim that they were instrumental in removing Arab power from Europe. Certainly they became the tools of the Inquisition in Spain, attacking Jews, Moslems and heretics and were used as a 'weapon' to eliminate all traces of anti-Catholic sentiment, belief and action.

Part of its power lies in the invention of a myth for its initiates, a fabricated pseudo-history used, in short, as a brainwashing technique. The story has it that the Garduna began after the first battle against the Arabs when the Holy Virgin of Cordova sought sanctuary with the Christians. God had been displeased with the Christians and had allowed Spain to be overrun by the Moors. The only people who survived, due to the mitigating tears of the Virgin, were an elite whose destiny was to retake the country. Their struggle was to last for 700 years. They hid themselves in the hills and formed a resistance group.

Apollinario, a hermit, lived a devout life worshipping the Virgin in a region of Spain called the Sierra Morena. She chose him as her messenger and appeared to the recluse to tell him that the Moors had been victorious due to a divine punishment. It was said that she had spoken to her son about the better qualities of the Spanish and that they should be given the chance of salvation. Christ agreed that Apollinario should be the one chosen for the task and that he should gather all the true Spaniards together and lead them against the enemy. Their rewards would be the possessions of the Moors.

The Virgin anointed the hermit and then presented him with one of her son's buttons, taken from his robes. The relic was claimed to possess such miraculous powers that even wearing one similar in form would protect its owner from death, the Moors and other heretics. The hermit then set about his task and formed the Holy Garduna.

That the Garduna had been given an order from on high to kill anyone who stood against them became an unquestioned tenet. If anyone criticised their power, then he was going against the word of God. This is an excuse that has been used in numerous cults – the idea that their activities, normally destructive, have been sanctioned by the 'highest authority' allows the leaders to get away with murder (literally), should they so desire. It is a powerful psychological ploy. If a member criticises the 'leader', he is flouting the word of God and can be threatened with eternal damnation.

Ferdinand the Catholic made great use of the Garduna in the Inquisition. Their reputation was legendary. In their blood lust against the Moors, they looted and burned indiscriminately. But it was not long before the warriors of the Garduna were looked on with suspicion. They had amassed a great fortune in their crusades and were not about to share it with anyone, least of all the king. They also set about removing anyone else they considered a threat, including Christian loyalists.

Moves were made against them but the Garduna remained under the protection of the Inquisition.

It was at this point that they became a proper secret society with nine degrees of initiation. These included the new initiates who were known as *chivatos* or goats and did all the dogsbody work. There were the *cobertas* or covers, women of a low moral fibre who were put to all kinds of uses, including luring men into ambushes. The *serenas* or sirens were more refined women and the *fuelles* or bellows made friends with potential victims. The grand master was known as the *Hermano Mayor* and his laws were absolute. These he issued to his *capataz* or regional bosses who would then utilise their *floreadores*, the muscle, and the *ponteadores*, the swordsmen, to enforce his will.

As well as being fighters the Garduna engaged in all kinds of other illegal activities. These ranged from kidnapping, assassination and the forging of documents to extortion, murder and enslavement. They were, of course, paid for all this and the monies raised were used to buy favours and corrupt those in power, particularly those, like judges, magistrates and prison governors, in the legal profession.

The Garduna continued to be a powerful force in Spain until 1822 when strong efforts were made to destroy it. As it had kept extensive records of its activities the incriminating evidence, including its long and profitable connection with the Inquisition, was there for all to see and this sealed the secret society's fate. The last recognised grand master was hung on 25 November 1822 in Seville's market square. But that was not the end of it. In the mid-nineteenth century the Garduna was known to be flourishing in South America and, as late as 1949, they were helping Nazis flee Europe. It is said that two rival Garduna orders now exist in Spain – one pro-church, the other a left-wing organisation intent on setting up a holy socialist state.

The Gnostics

During the first six centuries of the Christian era a number of sects flourished which came to be known under the collective title of the Gnostics, the *Knowers*. The Gnostics stood in opposition to *believers,* those for whom belief and faith were the most important qualities. To the Gnostics, belief was not enough and, although it was the mainstay of Christianity and other religions, they were not satisfied with blind faith. Into their version of Christianity they blended speculations from Pythagoras, Plato and other Greek and Oriental philosophers. Their studies were not narrowly confined and they absorbed all that was best from all the religions, ideas and teachings to which they had access. Their eclecticism brought them, in addition to the usual antagonism shown towards secret societies, unwarranted extra attention. They were accused of being Christian heretics, Jews trying to undermine Christianity or remnants of the Sun Worshippers of Persia. But they influenced many in Europe and formed the basis for many secret societies that followed.

The Gnostic teachers propagated the theory that humanity comes to its full potential by developing the mind. In short there must be a struggle towards *gnosis*. Yet this knowledge to which they aspired was of a mystical nature. The emphasis was not on the collection of ordinary facts but on a personal, mystical understanding of the world. Facts were part of the mundane material world which Gnostic teachers such as Valentinus argued was corrupt and evil.

The Gnostics believed themselves to be an intellectual elite and the knowledge for which they sought was only available to a minority, a few who were ready to receive it. Because of this they had many of the characteristics of a secret society including their own passwords and handshakes, in which only the palm was touched. (They were not particularly fearful of persecution but this was one method of maintaining a distance from all, in a spiritual sense, that was potentially harmful.)

Their main teachings were focused on a supreme power, which has no perceptible form and is, to all intents and purposes, invisible. This power can be contacted, through great effort, and, by this means, man can gain control over himself and discover his destiny. Numerous religious teachers of Gnostic persuasion claimed to be in contact with this higher power and all their various 'schools' used some form of initiation for the disciple. The Gnostics could communicate this secret only after the minds of the initiates had been purified, exercising the mind and body until 'terrestrial man' – the man of matter – becomes one of a mystically refined nature and is therefore able to become a 'vehicle' for this higher power. The initiate eventually becomes identified with the supreme power and elevates himself above crude matter and the rest of humanity who remain steadfastly unenlightened. This higher 'intelligence' was represented by the symbolic figure of Abraxas, his coded name being a representation of '365' – the number of days in a year. Abraxas wore a Roman soldier's armour or tunic and wielded a battleaxe in his right hand while, in his left, he carried a shield on which were often written the words IAO and SABOATH. Abraxas's head was that of a bird with an open beak while his legs were twin serpents. Beneath all this there was a thunderbolt. All of these images had hidden meanings. Abraxas's body stood for man, the bird stood for intelligence and the coming of light, the tunic represented the need for struggle and the battleaxe symbolised power and the dedication to Gnosis. The shield meanwhile meant wisdom and the serpent's insight.

The symbolism used with this teaching varied from Gnostic sect to Gnostic sect but there was always one constant element – the unconscious attainment desired by all. Gnostics claimed that within every human being there is an unfulfilled urge for a greater purpose but one that cannot be given proper expression because there is no social way in which that urge can be fulfilled. The Gnostics believed that this urge was in-built but it was only they who could show the way to achieve a state of completeness. The search for that completeness through anything else (love, business, theology, all those things that were rooted in the material world) is doomed to failure.

Of primary importance to the Gnostics were their practices, those used to produce enlightenment. The variations in the different sects mattered little. Discipleship, to them, was primary. The initiates must struggle and devote themselves to the supreme power. Secondly, they believed that there are two kinds of men in the world – those who are forever bound to the material world and those who can refine themselves in a spiritual sense. Gnostics would only accept acolytes from the second group. Thirdly, the methods employed to seek oneness with the divine power were varied and it was solely the decision of the teacher as to which route the initiate should take. For example, some Gnostic teachers taught that frenzy and excitement would produce the desired results, whereas many believed that meditation and fasting were the sole methods for reaching that higher mental state.

Because they drew on numerous sources for their beliefs, the Gnostics have often been termed pantheists. But this is not so. Neither, in a strict sense, can Gnosticism be considered a religion. The Gnostics stressed the importance of the individual over that of the group, whereas religion demands that the individual becomes part of a group, a faceless entity within a dogma. To the Gnostics it was more important to be 'enlightened'. Those who had achieved this state were more valuable, more refined and aristocratic. That is not to say that individualism was encouraged entirely. Some emphasis was laid on the individual contributing to the stability of the Gnostic group as well as to the larger community. This was one means by which they could survive. By adopting the doctrines of any religion and acquiescing to whatever politico-religious system prevailed at the time, they were able to flourish.

Like so many secret societies the Gnostics were accused of dubious crimes and irreligious behaviour by the Church. And, as has so often been the case, the accusations were based on wild fantasy and perceived threats. With little knowledge of what the Gnostics really believed, the Church had to create a whole panoply of crimes to tarnish their reputation. Some of the antagonism, however, was based on known and genuine heretical arguments advanced by the Gnostics. In the *Treatise of Resurrection*, the Gnostics taught that human existence is a kind of spiritual death and that the real resurrection comes when enlightenment is achieved in life – revealing true reality. When individuals realise this, they become spiritually 'alive' and can be 'raised from the dead'. In the *Gospel of Philip,* Christians who take the resurrection seriously are called ignorant – they have 'the faith of fools'.

> '*Those who say they will die first and then rise are in error*
> *They must receive the resurrection while they live …*'

The Gnostics are also associated with the Nag Hammadi Scrolls, fifty-two parchments found in Upper Egypt in 1947 and dated to around AD 350–400. Among these scrolls were the 'Gnostic Gospels' – works that had been ignored and indeed suppressed by orthodox Christians as heretical. As Knight and Lomas state in *The Hiram Key*: 'Had they not been, Christianity would have developed in a very different direction and the orthodox form of the religion that we know today might not have existed at all …' These kind of beliefs were powerful and threatened the authority of the Roman Catholic Church, which is founded on belief in the reality of Jesus's resurrection.

Gnostic belief is based on the principles of good and evil as conflicting forces and that a careful balance must be sought between them. This can only be achieved by a *Knower*, a Gnostic, the only one capable of predicting the outcome of an action and whether or not it will bring eventual good to a community or to the individual involved. There are echoes here of the Buddhist and Hindu idea of Karma – something that would not be alien to the Gnostics with their search for enlightenment in various and eclectic sources.

There were of course numerous variations on basic

Gnostic beliefs. Different factions placed emphasis on different aspects. The *Ophites*, for example, glorified the serpent that tempted Eve in the Garden of Eden because it brought forth knowledge into the world. The *Cainites* decreed that their followers should destroy everything which was a construct of the material world because matter was considered to be inferior. Basilides was a Gnostic leader who taught that Jesus did not die on the cross. (This is believed by a number of secret societies, including the Prieuré de Sion, and suggests that the Gnostics influenced many groups that followed in their wake.)

Gnosticism is still followed in various areas of the Middle East and Europe. The *Mandeans*, for example, a small community in Iraq, still follow an ancient form of Gnosticism using the same initiation rituals, which bear a striking similarity to those used in Freemasonry. Most contemporary Gnostics would subscribe to the ideas of Valentinus – that the world is more evil than good and that a man must purify himself by complete mental concentration. After death he will return to that from which he was severed, the supreme power, and will be reunited with his loved ones. Eventually, they hope all matter will be destroyed by fire.

The Golden Dawn

The Golden Dawn, or to give its full name, The Hermetic Order of the Golden Dawn was, in many ways, the most influential order to emerge from the occult revival at the end of the nineteenth century. It was made notorious by the activities of its most infamous member, Aleister Crowley, known as 'the Great Beast' or 'the wickedest man alive'. Other famous practitioners were W. B. Yeats, Algernon Blackwood and Arthur Machen.

Its overriding purpose was to create a system of 'working magic' brought together from a variety of disparate but extant sources. The Golden Dawn first saw the light of day in 1888 and was the creation of three Freemasons, Dr William Wynn Wescott, Dr William Robert Woodman and Samuel Liddell MacGregor Mathers. Wescott claimed to have secret documents, probably forged, that had once belonged to a German Rosicrucian order, in which five Masonic rituals were described. These were developed and expanded by Mathers who soon became the order's primary driving force, creating the rituals and laying out the structures in which the Golden Dawn should operate. It was divided into ten degrees, based on those found in the Sephiroth from the Qabalah (Kabbalah).

Mathers borrowed heavily from Eliphas Levi, Tarot,

Eastern Mysticism, Graeco-Egyptian and Jewish magic. He even brought in the peculiar Enochian language of the Elizabethan magus John Dee. By doing this, he gave the impression that the secret society had a provenance that could be traced into antiquity, particularly to the time of ancient Egypt.

Through ritual and careful study, members could pass through the degrees in temples named after the gods of Egypt on a quest to develop and enhance their higher selves and achieve a god-like state. This was done by identification with 'energies' and universal archetypes already present within the individual. All that was needed was a strong will to bring them into play. Mathers also claimed to be in contact with Magi or higher intelligences that operated in a secret order beyond the reach of everyone but him.

The Golden Dawn was not to last. Aleister Crowley was instrumental in its destruction, accusing Wescott of faking the Rosicrucian documents. Mathers left for Paris where he founded a new version of the group but that too was destined not to survive for very long. Yeats took over the running of the original Golden Dawn before A. E. Waite steered it in a Christian direction. The order finally ran out of steam in 1914. At its demise it had temples in Paris, Bradford, Weston-super-Mare, Edinburgh and Chicago. A number of still-existing occult groups claim a direct link to the Golden Dawn but, largely, this is in name only. Its modern equivalent is the OTO or the Ordo Templi Orientis. Aleister Crowley, the Great Beast, died in 1947, ending his days in a boarding house in Hastings, a somewhat surprising and banal setting for the death of someone allegedly in possession of great powers.

The Hell Fire Club

This once-notorious organisation was founded around 1750 by Sir Francis 'Hell-Fire Francis' Dashwood (1708–1781), a baronet, one-time MP, Chancellor of the Exchequer, Postmaster General and Treasurer to King George III. Dashwood had toured Europe as a young man and had grown to detest Roman Catholicism while developing a love of classical architecture and ancient mythologies. He was initiated into the Masons and, through his Jacobite connections – he was a spy for Prince Charles Edward Stuart – he became interested in Rosicrucianism. While he was in France he is said to have attended a Black Mass – more as a way to emphasise his dislike of Catholicism than because of a belief in Satanism.

Once, in Rome, during Holy Week, he disguised himself and entered the Sistine Chapel during one of the many scourging sessions that took place there. Just as the lights dimmed he set about the flagellants with a horse whip, convincing everyone that he was the devil himself come among them to administer his own discipline. All Dashwood was doing was expressing his contempt for religious hypocrisy, something he would continue to do throughout his life, often with a less than subtle humour. The rebellious aristocrat was a showman and he was certainly a rake and a ladies' man but he was also a witty and intelligent humanist.

On returning to England, Dashwood set up the Society of the Dilettanti, one of a series of clubs frequented by rakes and aristocrats that flourished in London at the time. This was followed by others called the Divan – a witty reference to his experiences touring the Ottoman Empire – and the Lincoln, a club in which tea parties and bowls were the principal interests. Then in 1746 he set up the Order of the Knights of St Francis who met at the George and Vulture pub in Cornhill. Five years later, Dashwood arranged a lease on the former 12th century Cistercian monastery Medmenham Abbey, near Marlow and not far from West Wycombe, the seat of his ancestral home, and set about moving the Knights of St Francis to a new location. At this time the Gothic revival was at its height and Dashwood converted the property to the tastes of that fashion but began adding overtly pagan elements to the reconstruction. He also added the legend 'Do as thou will' above the front door. He placed the 'guardians of secrecy', two statues – one of Angerona, the Roman goddess of silence and one of Harpocrates, the Egyptian equivalent – to his dining room.

Dashwood's taste for the pagan also extended to the decorations of his house, designed by Robert Adam. The west wing of the property was a facsimile of a temple to Bacchus and he made liberal use of images of Dionysus and Ariadne throughout. On its official opening Dashwood held a pageant, hiring actors dressed in animal skins and wearing ivy wreaths to play the parts of fauns, satyrs and nymphs. The garden of the house, again full of pagan imagery, was designed around the image of a naked woman with a swan-shaped lake that is supposed to symbolise the mythological Leda, who was impregnated by Zeus and produced two eggs, one containing Castor and Clytemnestra, the other Pollux and Helen. Dashwood's individual humour was further expressed in a statue of a naked Venus who was portrayed bending over so that any unwary visitor in the grounds often had the pleasure of walking into her buttocks.

In 1750 Dashwood extended a series of prehistoric caves beneath the nearby West Wycombe Hill and it was here that the Friars (the Hell Fire club was also known as the Friars of St Francis, the Monks of Medmenham and the Order of Knights of West Wycombe) moved for their secret rituals. Gossip, both in London and locally, was full of the wild orgies and debased practices of the Hell Fire Club.

The entrance to the caves was bordered by yew trees, symbol of immortality and often planted by the Druids near to their temples, and, inside, a low passageway led to numerous catacombs and the monks' cells in which they could entertain their female guests. The man-made system also featured a banqueting hall and an underground stream known as the Styx which had to be crossed to reach the Inner Sanctum in which, so rumour had it, the Black Masses were conducted.

There is much evidence to suggest that the caves themselves were a representation of the Mother Goddess in which the Hell Fire Club members were reborn, returning to ancient ideas of initiates seeking resurrection in this life, not after it. Whatever the nature of the ceremonies, the rumourmill was still grinding away and all the rumours were to the detriment of the order. It was claimed that Dashwood had prostitutes brought up from central London, via the Thames (which flowed nearby), to act as nuns in the Black Masses which were performed over the naked bodies of ladies of the aristocracy.

The reality was more prosaic and yet harked back to an older form of religion – that of the Druids. The presence of the yew trees would alert anyone in the know to the real activities that took place within the hallowed halls of the Hell Fire Club. The caves themselves pre-dated Dashwood by thousands of years and it is certain that the Friars of the Hell Fire Club were deliberately using a long-established pagan site to achieve a connection with the past. The site of St Lawrence's church, actually on the hill in which the caves existed, would have appealed to the prankster in Dashwood, giving him a further frisson of delight in the symbolic 'undermining' of the authority of the Church.

Some time before, Dashwood had joined the Society of Gentlemen of Spalding who had amongst their membership both Freemasons and Druids. Here Dashwood joined the Mount Haemus Grove of Druids who claimed a direct descent from a 13th century Oxford Grove. The Oxford Grove, in turn, had a supposed direct link to the ancient Mysteries of Ceridwen in North Wales. Dashwood had applied for a charter to run his own grove but the Druidic Council of Eleven refused him after they had heard the rumours of sexual antics taking place at Medmenham. This rejection did not stop him and he continued to pursue his goddess worship with gusto. The Friars themselves wore Druidic-style white robes with a silver badge that read 'Love and Friendship'. The whole Hell Fire Club, although it was not condoned by the contemporary Druidic cults, was nevertheless Druidic in nature, although it included rather more wine, women and song than were usual.

Perhaps to quell the rumours of devilish goings-on, Dashwood paid for the church of St Lawrence to be restored. Fittingly for such a self-proclaimed pagan, these would be no ordinary restorations. He based the reconstruction on the solar temple at Palmyra and there were other classical references in the form of olive branches, leaves, fruits, flowers and doves. A depiction of the Last Supper was painted on the ceiling which looks more like a Christian version of the Ancient Greek *agape* or 'love feast'. In the early Church, similar feasts were held before and after Communion but the rituals caused scandal and they were banned by the Council of Carthage in 397. Here is more evidence of Dashwood's sense of humour and his desire to criticise the established Church.

Further evidence that it was a Dionysian cult, rather than a Satanic one which took place within the caves of the Hell Fire Club can be found in the funeral rites of Paul Whitehead, one of the leading members of the order. In his will, Whitehead instructed that his heart and body were to be buried separately, the heart to be placed within an urn and interred in a mausoleum that had been erected above the caves. The urn, escorted by the Bucks Militia, Dashwood's private army, was walked three times around the mausoleum before being placed in a niche within. According to Eric Towers, Dashwood's major biographer, this is an updated version of the Dionysian ritual of dismemberment.

A number of famous names are supposed to have been members of the order, although we cannot be certain whether or not they were. These included William Hogarth, Horace Walpole, the Earl of Sandwich, Thomas Potter, the son of the Archbishop of Canterbury, John Wilkes, the Earl of Bute and the Prince of Wales. It is even claimed that Benjamin Franklin, a Freemason, attended a meeting or two.

Much of what went on in the caves remains pure speculation because no records exist beyond a few very ambiguous documents. In reality the members of the Hell Fire Club may just have been there for copious amounts of alcohol, the pleasures of the flesh and the enjoyment of a good time. In later years, Dashwood's house suffered at the hands of puritanical Victorians who defaced much of the pagan imagery in the building. Even the church of St Lawrence did not escape the activities of the pious vandals. In more recent times, certain evangelists have claimed, nonsensically, that the area is the centre of all evil in Britain. The truth is that Dashwood and his followers were not satanists. They were pagans who enjoyed a good time worshipping Bacchus and Venus – wine and women – and adding their own inspirations culled from the writings of Rabelais and seasoned by their particular sense of humour.

The reputation the Hell Fire Club earned was not deserved. Certainly its activities were bawdy and raucous and full of black humour – one initiate, forced to spout some inane profanity about the devil, was half scared out of his wits when a wild monkey was thrown onto his back – but it was not devil worship. The Hell Fire Club had more to do with the aristocrats letting off steam and doing what they pleased than with dark desires to serve the devil and bring down humanity. Its closest equivalent in contemporary secret societies is the Bohemian Grove – another club filled with establishment figures out to let down their hair.

The High Priesthood of Thebes

In all likelihood this was a completely bogus society. A detailed account appeared in Germany in the 18th century, claiming to reveal the details of the secret initiations of the Priests of Thebes and consisted of quasi-Masonic rituals. It outlines the stages of initiation from the first, via the Gate of Men, to the highest degree or the 'Propheta' in which all the secrets are told.

The Himalayan Masters

The Himalayan Masters are supposed to be benign and secret mystic rulers who, it is claimed, inhabit the 'roof of the world' and, through telepathy, dispense their mystical powers for the benefit of mankind. Secretive and remote, they shun normal life but allow seekers of true wisdom, on proof of their worthiness, to make contact with them. They then bestow their ancient wisdom on them. They are seen as a link between the profane world of ordinary men and the higher realms. They are staple characters, bordering on cliché, of adventure stories and films and, in all likelihood, the legend of these secretive figures has its origins in the misrepresented activities of Buddhist priests.

The Holy Vehm

Born out of the general anarchy that was Westphalia in the Middle Ages was a secret society determined to bring law and order back to the region which would claim to be a hundred thousand strong at its peak. This society was the Holy Vehm. The name Vehm is of uncertain origin. It could be derived from the Latin *fama*, meaning 'fame' or 'repute' or from the German *fahne*, meaning a flag banner or standard but its origins could equally belong in the Middle East. The initiates of the Vehm were called 'The Wise'. The word, pronounced fehm in German, is not dissimilar to 'fehm', the Arabic for wisdom. It may very well have come back with Germans involved in the Crusades. It was given the adjective 'Holy' because, in essence, it was a Christian order keen to promote the Ten Commandments and other Christian teachings.

The justice the Vehm meted out, at least in the early years of its existence, was swift and cruel but, like all secret societies, hearsay and rumour helped to exaggerate its darker aspects. One barbaric method of punishment alleged to have been used was an extraordinary machine, 'the Maiden's Kiss', that opened, much like an iron maiden, to admit its victim, who met his death by being chopped and diced with alarming alacrity by a series of brutal knives and spikes. What was left dropped into a nearby stream. Whether or not 'the Maiden's Kiss' really existed is open to debate. In all likelihood it owed as much to imagination as to fact. This form of 'justice', if it was truly in operation, was used against those the Vehm considered dangerous – those who practised heresy, theft, rape and highway robbery and those who turned from the Church. Women and children were exempt from the Vehm's particular form of legal redress, as were Jews and heathens whom the order considered simply beyond the pale.

The rank and file of the Vehm were known as the *Schoppen* or 'the ignorant'. Only after the initiation ritual were they known as 'the wise'. The ceremony itself consisted of the 'ignorant' kneeling before a tribunal of the Vehm and swearing an oath of service. The Vehm tribunals against the populace were held in large open areas and took place after the 'Secret Judges', who lived among the people keeping an eye out for trouble, made their reports about those individuals who had strayed from the law and singled out the miscreants by striking them with a white wand. Those who admitted their crimes were then told to leave the country within twenty-four hours. If a suspect was hit three times, he was taken away and hung and his body left to rot. Some 'Secret Judges' were human enough to try to warn those they were watching but, if they were caught, they would suffer the same fate as those they would normally condemn.

The courts themselves were initially greatly respected, despite their brutality. Most people accepted that rough times needed rough justice but eventually the Vehm became greatly feared and their support began to dwindle. The Vehm themselves did not help matters by initiating into their order people who would have been better candidates for hanging. The courts themselves were never formally abolished and were said to exist as late as the 18th century.

The Illuminati

With the Illuminati we have a secret society that appears to exist only as a heady fantasy in the fevered minds of conspiracy theorists who haul in all kinds of characters to perpetuate the fearful notion that all our lives are being controlled by a secret elite. Not only that but that this secret elite controls those who control us. The usual suspects, of course, make an appearance in the fantasies of these theorists. Henry Kissinger, for example, must spend all his waking hours attending every secret society meeting there is, even those with apparently conflicting goals. Probably his inclusion reflects the anti-Semitic ideas of some conspiracy theorists rather than Kissinger's obsession with dressing up and submitting to bizarre initiations.

These same conspiracy theorists have devised a 'pyramid of power' in which the Illuminati appear only some way up. Allegedly there are secret controllers above them in the form of a 'Committee of 300' with a single question mark at the pinnacle of the pyramid. Is there a room somewhere with a large curtain behind which a feeble man sits pulling levers all day? Is he the 'question mark'?

Supposedly, the Illuminati have infiltrated all the major secret societies from the Freemasons to the Skull and Bones at Yale and the Bohemian Grove. They have also been behind every war since 1800, controlling and manipulating world events for sinister purposes of their own. The theories make no logical sense. Kennedy surrounded himself with Bohemian Grovers so why would the Illuminati seek to assassinate him as some have suggested? Was Hiroshima bombed because it was a 'Christian' city or because there were armament factories there? War historians know the facts but the conspiracy theorists claim that the Illuminati were on an anti-Christian mission. Seen through the lens of that same extremist Christianity, the devil is said to be at work through the Illuminati and we will all be marked like the biblical beast with '666' – or, as the same hysterical critics claim, through microchip tagging. These ideas reveal a blatant and simple-minded paranoia and nothing else. Websites devoted to exposing the Illuminati are filled with this kind of irrational thinking. In many respects the Illuminati appear to be nothing but a useful fantasy, modern bogey-men created to assist the propagation of a fundamentalist Christian agenda. Is there any historical truth behind the fantasy?

In 1776, Adam Weishaupt, with the financial assistance of the house of Rothschild, set up a westernised version of a 16th century Muslim cult called *Roshaniya* – or the Illuminated Ones. The inner circle at this point included both the Marquis de Sade and Sir Francis Dashwood of 'Hellfire Club' fame. Weishaupt devised thirteen degrees of initiation and kept the power base in the top nine. Allegedly the Illuminati then set about infiltrating the Freemasons and every other organisation with which they had contact. Their whole purpose was to gain control over world affairs and bring about a New World Order. It is interesting to note that, from the very beginnings, the Illuminati embodied three primal Christian fears. A

Muslim cult, Jewish money and the devil in the form of Dashwood and his supposed satanic cult, the Hell Fire Club, combined to create a powerful and threatening force.

Weishaupt taught that everything was based around the number five, including human history. There were five stages in history – Chaos, Discord, Confusion, Bureaucracy and Aftermath in which society implodes and reverts back to Chaos again. With the Freemasons supposedly under his control, Weishaupt set about trying to destroy all of the social institutions of Europe. Critics of the Illuminati claim that the French Revolution was an experiment in '*Illuminism*' and that had God not intervened then all of Europe would have gone the same way.

Weishaupt's grand designs nearly succeeded but a courier, who was carrying vital documents written in an Illuminati cypher about the plans to subvert the Freemasons and the governments of Europe, was struck and killed by lightning. The Illuminati it is said, were forced underground but never went away and have managed to continue to spread their influence through the Freemasons who are now divided into two entities – ordinary Freemasonry and Illuminised Freemasonry, also known as the Grand Orient Lodges. Through their continuing influence, it is alleged, they play different factions against one another to create the desired changes – the overthrow of monarchies, the destruction of faith in God, the ending of nation states and patriotism and the dismantling of the social order. That all this represents a ludicrously naive and ignorant interpretation of history seems not to matter to the conspiracy theorists.

Another claim made of the Illuminati is that they hide themselves in plain sight. It is argued, for example, that the

Novus Ordo Seclorum seen on American currency translates as 'New World Order' and that this reveals the influence of the Illuminati. A moment's thought shows this to be nonsense. 'Novus' can also mean 'fresh' or 'young'. Ordo can also mean 'arrangement'. The motto can be paraphrased as the 'fresh new start' in which America threw off the shackles of the colonial British and came to a new arrangement of their own without a distant ruling power. Certainly many of the people who shaped the formative years of the United States and who signed the Declaration of Independence were Freemasons but does that really mean some shadowy figures calling themselves the Illuminati were secretly running the show?

It is also claimed that the Illuminati, as another way of hiding themselves in full view, construct buildings that look like owls. An owl or Molech (sometimes Moloch) is a symbol supposedly worshipped by the Illuminati. (Molech incidentally was an ancient fire god worshipped throughout Canaan and Phoenicia.) This claim also soon disintegrates under the impact of common sense. The 'architectural' owls can only be seen when viewed from a particular angle and after a great deal of imagination is brought into play. There are also claims that part of Washington DC's street layout resembles the image of an owl. The image is entirely invented by those who want to see it. Facial recognition is something that is hot-wired into the brain – we are almost programmed to see faces from infancy and that is why we see faces in the trunks of trees or in clouds and rock formations. The human brain is built for pattern recognition. The best example of this is the apparent face on Mars. No face exists and it is simply the play of sunlight on rock and the poor quality of the photography but our mind fills in the blanks. Carl Sagan in his exemplary book *The Demon-Haunted World* defines all this as the ill-thought out mental processes of the 'significance junkies' who seek meaning where none exists. The Washington owl falls into the same category.

It is also claimed that all kinds of media and government organisations which use, for example, the pyramid or pyramidal structure in their emblems are in the thrall of the Illuminati and that children's programmes are deliberately filled with subliminal messages or imagery that range from the cross of the 'dreaded' Knights Templar to the owls that appear in fantasy novels and films. The Harry Potter stories are the best modern examples. Should J. K. Rowling now be considered an instrument of the Illuminati?

It is alleged that supposed Illuminati figures like Rockefeller, Rothschild, Morgan, Roosevelt, Dulles and others were behind all large-scale world events from both World Wars and the Russian Revolution to every other major upheaval of the 20th and 21st centuries. Supposedly they do this to keep humanity in a state of division and fear as part of a strategy for global manipulation.

The same arguments used against the Illuminati and their supposed activities are true of the religion that is said to be the only redoubt against the 'satanic' figures of the Illuminati. In fact, more people have died as direct result of the ignorance, persecution and fear born of religion than through the alleged global plots of a secret society. More people are suppressed by religious extremism than by the machinations of a supposed secret elite. Conspiracy theorists are always seeking a new focus for their own fears and prejudices. Christian conspiracy theorists will see the devil and the Illuminati are just the 'devil' by another name.

The John Birch Society

The John Birch Society is a semi-secret fanatical right-wing group that was set up to fight Communism at the 'outbreak' of the Cold War. It is named after a United States Air Force captain called John Birch who was killed in 1945 by Chinese Communists. The Society considers him to be the first casualty of the Cold War and, more importantly, the first American to fall against Communism. The activities of the John Birch Society are now muted because of the collapse of the political ideology it was established to oppose but Marxist China still attracts its attention.

The Knights of Malta

Originally known as the Knights Hospitallers, they became
the Knights of the Holy Sepulchre, the Knights of St John of
Jerusalem, the Knights of Cyprus, then of Rhodes and finally
of Malta. They came into existence in the middle of the 11th
century with the aim of protecting Christian pilgrims on their
way to visit the Holy Sepulchre in Jerusalem. Italian merchants from Amalfi had built a Benedictine chapel and two
hospitals in Jerusalem and around this a military order grew
rapidly, to the extent that it received papal recognition and
exemption from tithes. Crusading nobleman and princes subsequently bestowed further gifts upon the site and the place
grew in size and scope.

After the death of its first rector, Gerard, in 1118 his suc-
cessor, a French nobleman named Raymond Dupuy, developed
the order along the lines that came to characterise it. It consisted of the Knights, to defend the Latin kingdom against the
Saracens, the Chaplains, to develop the religious aspects of the
work, and the Serving Brethren, to perform the day-to-day
labour. They all took the vows of the order and wore a black
robe with a cowl, with a white eight-pointed cross over the left
breast. The chief power was in the hands of the Grand Master
and it was he who appointed certain Knights, known as 'pre-
ceptors', to look after the order's interests around Europe.

The order was similar in many respects to the Knights Templar and, on the latter's suppression in 1312, many of their possessions were handed over to the Hospitallers. When the Holy Land was invaded by the Saracens in 1291, the Hospitallers moved their headquarters to Limasol in Cyprus and, in 1310, they captured the island of Rhodes and settled there, becoming known as the Knights of Rhodes.

There they remained until 1523 when, after a long siege by the Turks, they capitulated. From that point their fortunes began to fail. Like the Templars, they were viewed with jealousy and rapidly became *persona non grata* in many countries. Much of the animosity levelled at them came from the monarchs of Europe, including Henry VIII who confiscated their property in England in 1530. In the same year they moved once more and found refuge in Malta, ceded to them by the Holy Roman Emperor Charles V. It was not until 1798, when Napoleon invaded, that the Knights were forced to move when von Hompesch, the Grand Master, surrendered and promptly went into exile. The Knights were scattered throughout numerous European countries – the beginning of the majority of branches that exist today.

Today the Knights of Malta numbers some 11,000 and continue to defend the poor and the sick – although it has its critics, predominantly left wing. Many accuse it of having connections to extreme far right groups. The order maintains diplomatic relations with over eighty countries (excluding the UK and the US, probably because of the strong Protestant traditions in those two countries). Its controlling body, the Sovereign Council, meets every five years to discuss matters of importance, general policy and amendments to its statutes. Membership is limited to those who can trace a noble lineage and a family crest has to be presented by the candidate member. The organisation has Permanent Observer status at the UN General Assembly.

The Knights of Malta has a branch known as the Sovereign Military Order of Malta, in which the former CIA director William Casey and the fascist dictator General Franco were initiates. In the 1980s it helped right-wing insurgents in Nicaragua and El Salvador. It is claimed that George Bush Senior was also a member of this order when he was head of the CIA.

The Knights of St Columba

First set up in Glasgow on 5 October 1919, the Knights of St
Columba modelled themselves on their American equivalent,
the Knights of St Columbus who had been created in 1881 by
Father Michael J. McGivney. For the first year and a half the
order had no constitution and its ritual ceremonies were not
properly established but this did not stop it attracting several
hundred Catholics to its doors. Only allowing entry to prac-
tising Catholics, its aim was to advance the social and economic status of the faithful.

In the 1920s the order set up its first outpost in Liverpool
and not long after that it had reached London. This was the
period which saw its most rapid expansion, and up to 200
members at a time were often initiated into its ranks but by
the 1950s and 1960s the expansion had slowed. Initially the
order had been secretive and had a three-stage degree system but, in 1966, a simplified set of rituals was adopted and
the secret elements were removed. Today there are just two
'degree' levels – Membership on joining and Knighthood
after later elevation. There are around 8,000 members at
present throughout the country, divided into 340 Charter
Councils and 32 Provinces, and the order keeps its Supreme
Office in Glasgow.

The Knights Templar

At the beginning of the 12th century, nine French knights formed themselves into a band dedicated to protecting pilgrims on their way to the Holy Land. The were called Templars because their arms were stored in a building given to them by the abbot of the convent that stood on the site of the Temple of Solomon in Jerusalem. They wore a distinctive white tabard to which was later added a red cross on the left shoulder. In a little under two hundred years they became one of the most powerful institutions in Europe, with property in many European countries. They were initially praised as warrior monks but were soon the targets of envy and greed. At the time of their eventual downfall all kinds of erroneous accusations were levelled at them by the established Church and by those who were jealous of their power and wealth.

Soon after the formation of the order, Baldwin of Jerusalem, fearing Saracen attacks, realised that the Templars would make ideal allies so he arranged that they be recognised by the Holy See. On 31 January 1129, the Grand Master Hugh de Payens appeared before the Council of Troyes and the Templars were duly recognised. In the following year three hundred knights, allied with the Assassins, tried to take Damascus. There is much debate about the relationship between these two organisations but the fact that they were allies suggests they had more in common than is generally accepted. Certainly this alliance would come to haunt the Templars later when the bitter accusations of heresy began.

Even during the Crusades rancour against them was evident and there were claims that they were only fighting for their own self-interest. More importantly, it was said they were out to swell their own coffers and that the protection of Christianity came a poor second in their list of priorities. Many also accused them of being a law unto themselves. In 1155 the Templars gave their critics further ammunition by ambushing the fleeing Sultan Abbas who had been forced to leave Egypt after murdering the Caliph. The Moslems capitulated and the Templars sold the Sultan's son for 60,000 gold pieces. The fate of the Sultan himself remains a mystery.

At the time the Templars were busy developing their power base in the Middle East it is certain that they would have come into contact with certain mystery schools, including the Gnostics and the Manichae (the followers of Mani) and from these they would have taken much that was to become part of their secret lore. This too would play a part in their later downfall, as the 'secret knowledge' would be deemed satanic or devilish by their interrogators. In 1162 the Templars received the *Omne Datum Optimum*, a papal bull which consolidated their power and protected their secrets. But this too only served to fuel the envy of their enemies.

In 1184 Robert of St Albans left the Templars and led one of Saladin's armies against Jerusalem, which provoked a deeper mistrust of the order. Templars were accused of siding with the enemy, although this is not borne out by the facts. Saladin himself later stated that any captured Templars would be immediately put to death. After the battle of Hattin on

1 July 1187 Saladin captured 30,000 Crusaders, including a number of Templars who were all put to death with the exception of their Grand Master, Gerard de Ridefort. This battle marked the collapse of western power in the region and, although the Templars remained, their power base was now severely limited. When Jerusalem fell, they moved their headquarters to Paris, a more central location for their European activities.

While in Paris the Templars gave sanctuary to Philip the Fair, the French king and it is there, so the story goes, that he saw the inordinate wealth the supposed holy order possessed and decided to plunder it. There had been earlier attempts to attack the Templars. In 1208 Pope Innocent had publicly criticised the order and, forty years later, Henry III of England had also threatened them. But their downfall lay with Philip the Fair who had heard rumours that the Templars, frustrated in their efforts to win back the Holy Land, were about to try to overthrow both him and the newly-instated Pope Clement.

Rumours were already rife about the Templars and their supposed heretical behaviour. These had been spread by an ex-Templar, one Squin de Flexian, who drew up a great list of charges after he had been expelled from the order. In September of 1307 Philip sent sealed letters to all the regional governors in France, instructing them to act in a simultaneous strike on the Templars the following month. Exactly one month later nearly every Templar was arrested. All of them were subsequently tortured and dubious confessions were wrested from them to justify their destruction.

Some of the accusations levelled at the Templars were focused on their initiation ceremony in which they were said to state that Christ was not the saviour but a false prophet. It was said that they denied God and that they spat or urinated on the cross. They were said to worship the idol of a cat or a head called Baphomet and were also said to practise institutional sodomy. The Templars denied all the charges but fifty-four Knights who had defended the order were put to the flame.

Four years after this, in 1313, the Pope issued a bull stating that the order had officially ceased to exist. Jacques de Molay, the last Grand Master of the Templars, had been sentenced to life imprisonment but he and one of his closest colleagues, Guy of Auvergne, continued to protest their innocence. Fearing that this might rouse sympathy for the order, Philip had both men burnt at the stake.

Although there are a number of modern orders that bear the same name and claim links with them, the Templars are long defunct. In one sense they live on – in the places such Temple Meads, Templecombe and Temple Guiting that bear 'Temple' in their names. After their suppression, certain Knights travelled to Scotland where, it is claimed, they formed the basis of Freemasonry and eventually attached themselves to the Stuart cause. They were without doubt the most powerful military religious order of the Middle Ages and they continue to excite great interest, largely due to the claim that they were in possession of the treasure of the Temple of Solomon. What that treasure was, if it ever existed, is anyone's guess but one theory, the most popular, is that it was genealogical documents relating to the bloodline of Christ.

The Ku Klux Klan (KKK)

This originally referred to a secret and violent white-supremacist organisation founded by veterans of the Confederate Army in the Tennessee town of Pulaski in 1865. The original group opposed the reforms enforced on the South by Federal troops regarding the treatment of former slaves. It was originally set up as a social club with ornate rituals but its major aim was to terrify the black population of the area. Together with a related order called the White Camelias, it increased rapidly in size. Between them the two societies attempted to secure white supremacy in the South through murder and terrorism. By 1871, it had spread so widely and its activities had become so notorious that an Act of Congress was passed banning them. By 1880, the original KKK was a spent force and had all but disbanded.

The 'Klan' was highly organised and operated as an 'Invisible Empire' under a Grand Wizard. Each state was a 'Realm' under the control of a Grand Dragon and a number of counties made up a 'Dominion' ruled by a Grand Titan. Each county itself was a Province controlled by a Grand Giant with the Provinces themselves being divided up into 'Dens' each under a Grand Cyclops. Private members were known as Ghouls while minor officials went under names such as Nighthawks, Goblins and Furies.

In 1915 the KKK reared its ugly head again – this time in Atlanta, Georgia – and swept the South in the years following World War One. As before, it admitted only WASP Americans to its ranks. It took control of many elections, and politics in general in the South were affected by its activities but in the end its violent views brought about its own demise.

The KKK still exists today in a highly diluted form but its actions are muted and most members have drifted away to join the right-wing neo-Nazi groups that follow the same racist agenda.

The Mafia

The most famous criminal organisation in the world, popularised by films such as *The Godfather* series and on television by *The Sopranos*, the Mafia (or *Maffia*) began as a secret society in Sicily and soon outstripped its nearest rival the Camorra of the city of Naples. The *Omerta*, its code of honour, states that a Mafia member cannot seek redress in a court of law or give evidence before one. It also states that the law must be overridden wherever possible. Its strengths lie in the looseness of its organisation and, in reality, it is more an idea than a tightly constructed society. At its heart, especially in its initial stages in Sicily, is the idea that the people have control over their own affairs rather than being under the control of the recognised bodies of government. In the Mafia, the shadowy group has more respect than courts of law. By being diffuse and amorphous the Mafia is difficult for the same courts of law to control.

Protection money is levied from businesses using the time-honoured method of blackmail and the vendetta is reserved for those who denounce members of the fraternity. Outside of Italy the Mafia is strongest in the United States where it is known as *Cosa Nostra* or 'Our Thing' and it is particularly active in New York, Las Vegas and Chicago. In New Orleans it was known as *The Black Hand*. The Prohibition Era in America saw the Mafia rise in prominence and the authorities, inadvertently, raised their power base and profile, establishing them forever as a powerful entity within the country.

The Society of Merchant Venturers

For eight hundred years the wealthy and educated elite of Bristol have been shaping that city's fortunes in the guise of the Merchant Venturers, a publicity-shy organisation that continues to keep its activities secret. Its headquarters are on the Bristol Downs and its current 'Grand Master' is Denis Burn. In the past members secured their money through shipping and the slave trade but in more recent times the business has been more of a legitimate nature. They have a reported one hundred million in charitable trusts, money which is used to fund private schools, care for the elderly and other works. In the past this money has built almshouses, bridges and familiar local landmarks around the city. Membership is through invitation only and is only open to those who have succeeded in the field of business. In recent times the Merchant Venturers have become less camera shy. Because of the usual accusations of secrecy and their being an apparent undemocratic control within society they have taken steps to become a bit more open.

The Odd Fellows

Once a semi-secret society with benevolent ambitions, the Oddfellows has a history that dates back to 1745, although members claim it has origins that date back to the exile of the Israelites from Babylon in 587 BC. Many of these same exiles banded together for protection and further survived the fall of Jerusalem in AD 70. A lodge of Oddfellows was supposedly set up by Roman legionaries in Britain in 100AD. The society's own legend then states that the Order of Oddfellows was taken to Spain by the Romans and, from there, spread into Portugal and France.

In the 12th century Jean de Neuville re-introduced it into Britain and, with five of his fellow French knights, established the Grand Lodge of Honour in the City of London. The foundation of the Order of Oddfellows in England was thus established.

It weathered the storms of the Sedition Act and flourished, finding new strength in 1813 as the Independent Order of Odd Fellows in Manchester. It has become one of the greatest of the 'Friendly Societies', spreading across Europe and to North America. Although it is an organisation open to all, it still uses Masonic titles such as Grand Master.

Opus Dei

Opus Dei, the Latin for '*God's Work*', is a fundamentalist, some say fascistic, organisation that operates within Roman Catholicism. Officially it is considered to be part of the Catholic Church and Opus Dei claims that it has no separate identity but there is much to suggest that it is, in reality, a self-governing body. The order was established in 1928 and has grown to include approximately 80,000 members in Europe and North and South America, predominantly in countries where the Catholic faith is at its strongest.

Recently Pope John Paul II, much to the consternation of its critics, approved the controversial canonisation of the order's Spanish founder, Josemaria Escriva de Balaguer. De Balaguer, judging by his writings, was indeed a fascist, who condemned everything not Catholic or right wing and had a particular antagonism towards liberals and women. A devious and socially snobbish man, he had connections with the Franco dictatorship and, together with most Spanish church-men, he sided with the Nationalists against the Spanish Republic in the 1930s. Republican militias set about murder-ing thousands of priests. De Balaguer himself had to flee for his life. With this background it is hardly surprising that an-tipathy towards the left was a driving factor in his politics. He also had a strong sympathy with Hitler and has been famously quoted as arguing that the Nazi dictator would save Christianity from Communism. (Communism is not always directly mentioned in the literature of Opus Dei but, according to many ex-adherents, anti-Communism is everywhere in the organisation.)

Opus Dei has often been described as a kind of Catholic Freemasonry and critics accuse it of being secretive and overtly manipulative but de Balaguer preferred to use the word 'discreet'. As in Freemasonry, membership is by invitation only but there the similarities end. Indeed de Balaguer has been quoted as saying that Freemasonry is nothing short of the work of the devil. In many ways Opus Dei more resembles a cult and there are claims of brainwashing and religious indoctrination from those who have fled its confines.

It is a strong proponent of deeply conservative Catholic values, including a firm opposition to abortion and artificial contraception. It also claims a unique status for Roman Catholicism – that it is the true church and all else is just flummery and deceit. Its relationship with Pope John Paul II has been hotly debated. One of the pontiff's favourite theologians, Hans Urs von Balthasar, described Opus Dei as a 'concentration of fundamentalist power in the Church'. Yet the Vatican's press spokesman, Joaquin Navarro-Valls, is a member of Opus Dei so a conflict of interests is inevitable.

Is it really fascist? Opus Dei's relationship with Franco was always ambiguous and, although certain of the regime's senior officials were members, a faction of Opus Dei engineered separation from the Spanish dictator and, by doing so, helped to prepare the way for Spain's burgeoning democracy in a post-Franco world. On the other hand, Opus Dei's critics reach for de Balaguer's manifesto, called *The Way*, which certainly embodies elements of fascist ideology. There is the fundamentalism, the intolerance towards other religions, the undemocratic structure of the order and its commitment to following orders blindly. There is danger inherent in the psychological control the order exercises over its members through the 'weekly chat' (in which they have to tell the innermost details of their souls to their spiritual leaders) and in the aggressive and manipulative way they try to catch new members. Combine this with the fact that they do not reveal their true goals, and keep a lot secret from the public, and with de Balaguer's insistence on a ruling elite and it has all the hallmarks of a cult built around a charismatic leader.

Like most cult leaders, de Balaguer also said that people are not even equal in the eyes of the god they worship. Priests are more valuable than the initiates themselves. In *The Way* whole chapters express the need for strong leadership and suggest that there are people who are inherently superior; an elite that have all the answers and should be blindly followed. This is alarmingly reminiscent of both Hitler's Aryan dreams and the familiar patterns that are to be found in all secret societies.

Opus Dei members, it is alleged, had to treat de Balaguer almost as if he were God himself and even today members still write letters to him, although he has long since died. No other religions are mentioned in his book. There are no others, outside Catholicism, worth considering. However, it is claimed that he called Queen Elizabeth, head of the Anglican Church, 'this daemon' and certainly he loathed other Christian religions such as Protestantism with a passion. His attitude to non-Christian religions can be judged from the fact that he often used the names of battles fought by Christians against Moslems as metaphors for victory.

Accusations of Opus Dei's influence on Roman Catholicism are often hard to ignore. How much part did it play, for example, in the failure to speak out against the Nazi government during the Second World War. The criticism has been further aggravated by the Pope's beatification of de Balaguer, which has undoubtedly given a very bad signal to the outside world. Like most other clandestine organisations, the order has been also accused of infiltrating the mass media to further its policies of indoctrination. In 1979 the then head of Opus Dei had drawn up some statistical material for the Vatican, material that was soon made public by 'certain indiscretions' and revealed that the order had 479 members in various universities, 604 in newspapers, 52 in radio and television stations, 38 in news and advertising agencies and 12 in film production companies. Opus Dei has also recently infiltrated such arenas as public Internet chat rooms with their 'agents', and members of Opus Dei are involved in right-wing politics, trying to secure influence within institutions such as the European Union, the FBI, CIA and numerous Governments. Most importantly, the order's fundamental, messianic aim is to create a world in which everyone is a Catholic.

The Order of the Peacock Angel

Not known to exist anymore, the Order of the Peacock Angel was brought to London in 1913 by a Syrian whose name remains a secret until after initiation. The cult was split into *halkas* (lodges) and each had a minimum of seven members. It had its roots in Sufism and Arab numerology, and also had connections to the Yezidis of Kurdistan. Followers worship the snake and the peacock, both of which are symbols of power. It is open to men and women with the male objectives being fraternal fellowship and the sharing of ecstatic experiences.

The Ordines

The Ordines is a cabal that has emerged in the conspiracy theories recently and is sometimes said to be the undefined power base at the top of the 'global elite pyramid' – the question mark mentioned earlier. There is little information about them, but the rumours suggest that they are the 'select few' who use the Illuminati as the medium through which their commands are acted out. (This is to assume, of course, that the Illuminati are a real force and not just the creation of conspiracy theorists.) They are said to number just three so that if a decision has to be made there is never a hung vote. They are represented by the image of the Golden Ball – or sun sphere. The Golden Ball is modelled on the one above the Custom House in Venice and the one seen on the spire of the church of St Lawrence, restored by Sir Francis Dashwood of the infamous Hell Fire Club. In this globe there are seats for three people.

The Illuminati, or 'illuminated ones', assuming they exist, may be revealing the real power that controls them in their name. The sun, of course, is the source of all life on the Earth. The symbolic use of the Golden Ball follows a direct route from the Hell Fire Club and Freemasonry to the Illuminati and hence the Ordines. Conspiracy theorists see the pyramidal shape of many company logos as evidence that the

Illuminati are the power behind the throne. Some of these brand names incorporate an eye or a flame – for example, the torch held by the woman in the Columbia Pictures logo. This torch, it is said, represents the Ordines.

P2

On 26 May 1981 the Italian government collapsed after scandalous revelations of its infiltration by members of an illegal Masonic lodge called 'P2', or 'Propaganda Due', which had been created in the 1960s. Less than two months later, the country banned secret societies. P2, a breakaway lodge of the Grand Orient of Italy, consecrated in 1895, achieved notoriety in the 1980s through the links it created between the Italian government and the CIA-backed Gladio campaign, responsible for a series of bombings that were blamed on the left. There were deep connections to the Vatican's Banco Ambrosiano. The bank's directors, including the infamous Roberto Calvi, known as 'God's Banker', were involved in laundering billions in Mafia funds for right-wing groups like *Solidarity*. In 1982, Calvi was found hanging beneath Blackfriars Bridge with bricks and concrete in his pocket, suggestive of a ritualistic Masonic death.

Running the entire operation was a man called Lucio Gelli who was heavily involved in varied aspects of organised crime. He had fought with Franco's Fascist forces in Spain, before fighting for the SS on the Eastern Front. Not long after the war, he became a 'democrat' and a virulent anti-communist. Not long after that, the CIA began collaborating with him in the Gladio operation.

While under Gelli's Grand Mastership, it is rumoured, P2 operatives murdered Pope John Paul I because he threatened to reveal their activities. The Vatican continues to refuse all demands for a full inquiry into the Pope's death, with the result that whispers about its complicity in the affair continue to circulate. P2 applied its machinations from the world of business to that of politics to such a corrupt level that the Masonic hierarchy had no choice but to shut the lodge down. Lucio Gelli was then promptly expelled from a bruised and battered Freemasonry, which had once more come under the spotlight of critical scrutiny – something it could ill afford.

P2 had branches in a number of South American countries including Argentina and Venezuela but there were also affiliates in the United States, Switzerland, France and Cuba. It formed a direct link between the Vatican and the CIA but rumours abounded that the lodge was controlled by more sinister powers. Both the American Mafia and the KGB were said to be the secret controllers of P2. Some have even suggested the Prieuré de Sion was involved. A journalist called Mino Pecorelli, a P2 defector, pointed the finger at the CIA but he was found murdered.

The plot thickened after the police raided Gelli's house and found a great deal of documentation in which organisations such as Opus Dei and the Sovereign and Military Order of the Temple of Jerusalem – a group who claim direct descent from the Knights Templar but who have only existed since the early 19th century – were mentioned. The modern Order of the Temple of Jerusalem bears no relation to the original Templars and in many cases is at political odds with the causes of the earlier order. In any event, would the Knights Templar really have an ally in the form of the Roman Catholic Church and the Vatican?

Prieuré de Sion

That there was an historical Order of Sion is indisputable but whether it has anything to do with the Prieuré de Sion made famous in *The Holy Blood and The Holy Grail* by Baigent, Leigh and Lincoln is questionable. An Order of Sion existed up until the 17th century, at the latest, while a Prieuré de Sion existed from 1956 to 1984 but, if the two societies have or had any connection, then there is little evidence of it. The latter was the creation of one Pierre Plantard de Saint-Clair, a right-wing fantasist who, according to certain documents, is the lineal descendant of Dagobert II and therefore of the Merovingian dynasty of French kings and hence, it is claimed, of the bloodline of Christ. What makes academics suspicious is that the records for Plantard's Prieuré de Sion date back only to 1956.

The Order of Sion legend has it that a group of Calabrian monks left the Belgian Abbey of Orval in 1090 and helped the election of Godfroi de Bouillon as King of Jerusalem (he refused the position), convinced that he was a descendant of King David and Solomon. Godfroi, in recognition of their actions, granted them an abbey on Mount Sion. It is also claimed that the Order of Sion and the Order of the Temple (Poor Knights of the Temple of Solomon or later the Knights Templar) were one organisation under one leadership.

Documents appear from 1116 in which with the order's name includes a charter for their first European base in Orléans.

The order also had links with the noble families of France that claimed a direct descent from the Merovingians who had ruled the country between the 5th and 8th centuries. The Sion's first independent Grand Master was John de Gisors who was related to Hugh de Payen (also known as Hugues de Payn), the Templar Grand Master. The Order of Sion name continued to appear on documents in the 12th and on up to the 17th century, after which it disappeared until it resurfaced under the guise of the Prieuré de Sion in the 20th century and the leadership of Pierre Plantard de Saint Clair who claimed he was related to the Saint-Clair family which had had connections with the order in its early days.

According to Baigent, Leigh and Lincoln the Prieuré had connections with elusive groups such as the Rosicrucians, the heretical clerics of the Compagnie du Saint Sacrament and the Freemasons. What brought the Prieuré to the attention of the world, via the book *The Holy Blood and The Holy Grail* and later *The Messianic Legacy,* was its apparent connection with the activities of Bérenger Saunière, a priest based in Rennes-le-Chateau in south-west France. While renovating his church, he is supposed to have discovered hidden documents in a pillar that were clues to a great and mysterious treasure. The story goes that he came into great wealth and was able to restore the church to his own specifications and to live a life of relative luxury despite being a poorly paid churchman. The money was allegedly paid to him by the Church Establishment to enforce his silence over the mystery he had uncovered. The solution to the same mystery had been hidden away in certain paintings by various artists over the centuries, including Poussin and Leonardo Da Vinci who, it is claimed, was once Grand Master of the Prieuré de Sion.

The secret was, in essence, the notion that Jesus Christ had sired children and his bloodline had been preserved by inter-marriage with the Merovingians. Pierre Plantard de Saint-Clair claimed that the modern Prieuré de Sion were keepers of that knowledge and protectors of the holy bloodline. The ultimate goal was to unite Europe under one monarchy, one that was based on the Holy Grail – the bloodline of Christ. The jury until recently was still out as to the authenticity of the modern Prieuré de Sion although it looks increasingly likely that it is a bogus organisation as the 1956 documents held in Paris are now considered to be fakes.

The Rosicrucians

> *'As for Rosycross Philosophers,*
> *Whom you will have to be but sorcerers,*
> *What they pretend to is no more*
> *Than Trismegistus did before,*
> *Pythagoras old Zoroastra,*
> *And Apollonius their master.'*
>   Butler: *Hudibras*, Pt. II, iii

Mystery has surrounded this secret order since it first announced its presence via a German pamphlet of 1614 entitled *Fama Fraternitatis of the Meritorious Order of the Rosy Cross*. In this tract the Rosicrucians claimed that they had been in existence for more than a hundred years prior to their breaking cover and were a fraternity established by one Christian Rosencreutz (Rosy Cross) in 1459. When the *Fama Fraternitatis* was published there was no evidence beyond this work that anyone called Rosencreutz ever existed. He seems to be more of a mythical or allegorical character than an actual individual. Nonetheless 1614 marked the point at which Rosicrucianism entered the collective consciousness.

Christian Rosencreutz, the *Fama Fraternitatis* stated, was a German nobleman who had been sent to a monastery in 1378 to learn Latin and Greek. He was taken to Cyprus by a monk who promptly died, leaving Rosencreutz alone. It is said that he then travelled to Arabia (a doubtful destination for a Christian at the time) and in particular to a place called *Damcar* – but no such place ever existed. He then studied in Fez and in Egypt, finally bringing the knowledge he gathered there back to Europe.

Other documents soon followed, all claiming to be the works of the order. These included *Confessio Fraternitatis R.C. Addressed to the Learned of Europe* (Cassel, 1615); *Chymical Marriage of Christian Rosencreutz* (Strasbourg, 1616); *Perfect and True Preparation of the Philosophical Stone, according to the Secret of the Brotherhoods of the Golden and Rosy Cross* (Breslau, 1710 – this also contains the laws of the order); and *Secret Symbols of the Rosicrucians of the Sixteenth and Seventeenth Centuries* (Altona, 1785–88). Whether all of these documents were genuine is a matter of fierce debate as a number of imitation Rosicrucian orders emerged shortly after the *Fama Fraternitatis*, all claiming, of course, to be the original source for the material.

The Rosicrucians were represented in these documents as being skilled in the Hermetic arts, including the transmutation of metals, power over elemental spirits and the knowledge of magical signatures – the *signatura rerum* of Paracelsus. They could go without food and water and it was claimed they could make themselves invisible on a whim. It has often been suggested that the word 'Rosicrucian' does not derive from the Rosy Cross or from the surname of their supposed founder but stems from *ros crux* or 'dew cross'. Dew was hailed as the most potent solvent of gold. In alchemy the cross is the symbol of light because of the idea that any image of the cross contained the three Latin letters 'LVX' – 'lux' or light.

In the cryptic and often baffling language of alchemy 'lux' is the menstruum of the red dragon (corporeal light) and this light, when properly 'digested' in dew, produces gold. Rosicrucians were therefore 'they who used dew for digesting light to find the philosopher's stone' – the miraculous substance that would convert all base metals into gold.

The order also aimed to institute a major overhaul of the arts and sciences of the time, particularly alchemy (the most famous Rosicrucian pursuit) and medicine. Oddly, the Rosicrucians invited all 'students of nature' to join them in their work but left no clues as how to find them. This persuaded many critics that the order was nothing but an elaborate hoax aimed at the weak-minded. At the same time, great controversy developed in Germany as rival publishing houses began printing pamphlets with opposing stances on Rosicrucian thought. Among those defending the secret order were Michael Maier in Germany and Robert Fludd, Thomas Vaughan and John Heydon in England. Those against were Johann Valentin Andreii and Andrew Libavius. Yet no one was sure if the Rosicrucians really existed as a genuine organisation. The authorship of the original manifestoes was generally attributed to a character called Andrea. It is certain that he wrote the *Chymical Marriage of Christian Rosencreutz* but the question of authorship of the others has taxed many an inquirer in the order right up to the present day and as yet no real consensus of opinion has been reached. What is known is that he, as a Lutheran, spread his Protestantism through these documents but soon after Roman Catholics made their presence felt in the Rosicrucian debate and begin to shift the emphasis towards their faith. Andrea promptly denounced them and set up a new order called the *Fraternitas Christi*, then another called the *Blue Cross*. (It is interesting to note in passing that Martin Luther's heraldic image consisted of a rose and a cross. Is this the true source of Rosicrucianism?)

The rose and the cross were also important symbols for other mystical schools at the time, including the Sufi who had an order called *The Path of the Rose*. The Arabic *Path of the Wird* was represented by the image of a rose. This suggests that Rosicrucianism may have simply been a cocktail of ideas sourced from a number of secret mystery schools active at the time.

A Rosicrucian order had been founded in London as early as the 17th century and included Elias Ashmole (founder of the Ashmolean Museum in Oxford) as one of its members but it claimed to be only interested in books and antiquarianism. During the Revolution, Rosicrucianism flourished in France and in England it again took hold somewhere at the beginning of the 19th century. Robert Wentworth developed a *Societas Rosicruciana in Anglia* in 1857 as an offshoot of Freemasonry. Later in France, Claude Debussy was introduced to the order by his fellow composer Erik Satie and such artistic luminaries as Jean Cocteau and Pablo Picasso were involved in it.

Today the original order, if it ever existed, is defunct. A number of organisations have sprung up to fill the void, adopting the same name. The most famous is AMORC (Ancient Mystical Order Rosae Crucis), familiar from magazine adverts and based in the United States. The truth is that it has little to do with Christian Rosencreutz and the Rosicrucians of the past.

The Royal Antediluvian
Order of Buffaloes

Although it is not, strictly speaking, a secret society, much of the development of the Royal Antediluvian Order of Buffaloes occurred along Masonic lines and it has taken on much of the regalia and ceremony of the Freemasons. The earliest date for a RAOB lodge is 1822 at the Harp Tavern on Great Russell Street, not far from the Drury Lane theatre, and it was created by theatre stagehands and technical staff who were denied membership of the City of Lushington, a kind of closed shop organisation for actors. The City of Lushington was arranged in wards with a Mayor (Grand Master) and various Aldermen. There were also lesser officers with City as a prefix such as City Barber or City Taster. The City Taster had the duty of testing the ale that was to be con-sumed within a lodge session. If the beer failed to come up to scratch, the landlord was fined two barrels of beer.

Initially the technicians had been invited as guests to join the City of Lushington but soon their presence was not wel-come. Instead they moved to develop their own select gath-ering. As they toured the country, numerous other lodges were set up in towns and cities. The theatre critic Pierce Egan claims that it was the well-known eccentric Joseph Lisle and a man called William Sinnett who were responsible for the spread of the Buffaloes.

The 'Antediluvian' used in the name was intended both to refer to the age-old impetus to help the poor and needy that was their raison d'être and to impress others into thinking the order was older than it was. The 'Buffalo' comes from a ballad, 'We'll Chase the Buffalo', that was sung by members at the original meetings and was later promoted by Pierce Egan in his book *Tom and Jerry*. The 'Royal' part has its own history. The Seditious and Riotous Assembly Acts of 1799 had a great impact on all societies and orders. Like the Masons, the RAOB came under direct scrutiny from the authorities. They added 'Loyal' to their name to allay fears that the order was in any way a threat to the crown. Over the years this was corrupted to Royal. A royal charter has never been granted to the Buffaloes but, after the Royal Warrant Act of the early 1900s, which decreed that permission had to be sought by any organisation for the continued use of 'Royal' in its name, it was agreed that the Buffaloes could continue using it.

The first lodge was known as the Mother Lodge from which all advice and regulations flowed. Soon there were District Grand Lodges and Provincial Grand Lodges and then, in 1866, a Grand Primo Lodge was instituted to control all rules and regulations. Today the order is structured along Masonic lines with a three-tiered system of Minor Lodges, Provincial Grand Lodges and the Grand Lodge.

The RAOB has four degrees – First Degree, known as 'Kangaroo', Second Degree or 'Certified Primo', Third Degree or 'Knight Order of Merit' and Fourth Degree or 'Roll of Honour'. In the early days many Masons had become members and their influence can be seen in the regalia and the rituals still used by the RAOB. In fact many Freemasons continue to belong to the Buffaloes.

The Shriners

At a special table on the second floor of the Knicker-bocker Cottage, a restaurant at 426 Sixth Avenue, a group of men used to meet on a regular basis. They were all Masons but they often discussed the idea of a new fraternity in which fun and fellowship would be the order of the day rather than ritual. Two of the regulars, Walter M. Fleming, M.D., and William J. Florence, an actor, decided to pursue the idea.

Some time later, while in Marseilles, Florence was invited to a party given by an Arabian diplomat where he saw an elaborate musical comedy. As its finale, the guests were initiated into a secret society. Hastily taking notes, Florence realised that this should be the basis for the new fraternity. On returning to New York, he told Dr. Fleming who took the ideas and developed them into the *Ancient Arabic Order of the Nobles of the Mystic Shrine* (A.A.O.N.M.S.). The initials can spell out 'A MASON' which is doubtless not a coincidence.

Fleming came up with the rituals, designed the emblem and ceremonial costumes, devised a salutation, 'Es Selamu Aleikum!' and decided that members should wear a red fez with a black tassel. The Jewel of the Order was to be a Crescent, the most valuable being made from the claws of a Royal Bengal Tiger.

In the New York City Masonic Hall on 26 September 1872,

the first Shrine Temple in the United States was instituted and Dr. Fleming proposed that this first Temple be named Mecca. The original 13 Masons of the Knickerbocker Cottage lunch group were also named as Charter Members. By 1878, there were 425 Shriners in 13 Temples based in New York, Ohio, Vermont, Pennsylvania, Connecticut, Iowa, Michigan and Massachusetts. During the 1880s the Shriners continued to grow in strength and, by the time of the 1888 Annual Session in Toronto, there were 48 Temples with 7,210 members, located throughout the United States and Canada.

The Shriners engage in pageantry and are often seen in small cars or on horseback in parades, sporting their distinctive fez headgear. They raise great amounts of money for charities and their own Shriners Hospitals. They are based largely in North America. They follow Masonic traditions but tend to be a more visible presence than their fraternal brothers in Freemasonry.

The Skull and Bones

The Skull and Bones was founded at Yale in New Haven, Connecticut in 1832 and is the oldest and most influential of the seven secret societies there. Only the Scroll and Key can claim near equal status. In 1856 it was officially incorporated under the less dramatic name of the Russell Trust Association. The fraternity, like the others at Yale, serves to groom young men for careers in government, law, the intelligence services and banking and has done for 170 years. It is a redoubt of those Anglo-Saxon values which many claim are at the heart of the US government's idea of a New World Order and the American century. There are numerous Skull and Bones members among America's elite. Their aim, it is claimed, is to increase the power of the United States on the world stage by using the idea of constructive chaos – setting both allies and foes against one another – and by constantly sending out mixed policy messages while keeping their true intentions secret. Universities like Harvard and Princeton have similar secret societies but their influence pales into insignificance in comparison with the infamous activities of their Yale rivals.

According to some the Skull and Bones has an underground connection with two other societies, which were founded at the same time. Under the fraternity's emblem, the skull and crossbones, there is the number 322 and this refers, supposedly, to the year of its inception and its status as the second lodge in the triumvirate which includes one in Germany and another at a second, unnamed American university.

At any one time there are only around 600 members and, since its inception, the Skull and Bones has initiated only 2,500 into its brotherhood. A number of different stories about its origins have been perpetuated, apparently deliberately by those involved. The first version has it that the Skull and Bones is an offshoot of British or Scottish Freemasonry – the skull and bones is a common symbol. The second claims that it has a Germanic origin in a number of right-wing secret societies that flourished in the early 19th century and the third is that the society is a purely American invention, albeit one that borrows heavily from Masonic ritual.

Its roots and later financial sustenance can be traced back to the opium trade carried out by the British East India Company, controlled in its early years by the Baring Brothers Bank, which was at full power when the Treaty of Paris was signed to end the American War of Independence. The British financial house of Rothschild took over the running of the British East India Company and began sponsoring many of the New England families who had sided with the mother country during the Revolution. These families, such as Cabot, Coolidge, Lodge, Perkins and Russell (the Russell Association), all grew rich running fleets of ships. They subsequently set up the Bank of Boston and the United Fruit Company but, more importantly, they were the founding families of the Skull and Bones. These same families, now much intermarried, still hold sway even today over entry into the secret society. There is a core group of between twenty and thirty prominent names including, as well as those already mentioned, Taft, Whitney, Phelps and Adams. A second wave of new blood came later in the form of other wealthy families such as Rockefeller, Pillsbury and Davison.

The early guiding light was William Huntington Russell who was valedictorian of his class in 1833 and, more importantly, saw himself, as well as his fellow Skull and Bones colleagues, as the elite of the elite. He believed that because they were of Puritan pilgrim stock then they were chosen by God and destined to rule America. The same sort of like-minded individuals had been instrumental in setting up Yale three generations before and indeed many of the university's graduates became active in the American Revolution.

Initiation into the order is called 'tapping' and is conducted by 15 senior classmen who are already members. They select 15 likely candidates to become initiates into the Skull and Bones for the following year. Beyond the importance of family ties, the selection process is based on the 'Three Ordeals', which are used to ascertain the candidate's suitability. The first of these is 'boarding school'. It is vitally important which one the candidate has attended. The preferred schools are Groton and the two Puritan Calvinist-backed Phillips Academies where education is predominantly Anglophile in nature. Secondly, there is 'nature' – the proposed candidates are judged on their skills in hunting and other outdoor pursuits. The third is 'war' and the candidate's desire to enter some form of military service after graduation – the US Navy is the preferred option.

The senior 'Bonesmen' proceed to the room of the selected candidate and bang loudly on his door. The new recruit is tapped on the shoulder and asked, 'Skull and Bones, do you accept?' If he does, he is handed a scroll sealed with black wax and a ribbon, bearing a skull and crossbones image and the number 322. This scroll contains the time and place for the initiation, which is usually 'The Tomb', the on-campus head-quarters of the Skull and Bones. The initiation ritual is only briefly mentioned in occasional documents but doubtless it resembles other such ceremonies in secret societies. The candidate is carried to the centre of the room, chanted over and is reborn or resurrected into his new life. The variation is the use of a bone with the new initiate's name on it that is added to a pile at the beginning of every meeting.

Within the Tomb there is a secret room or vault, which carries above its entrance the words, 'Who was the fool, who was the wise man, beggar or king? Whether poor or rich, all's the same in death,' written in German. Supposedly this is part of a Masonic ritual from Germany. This has led many critics to believe that the Skull and Bones is a neo-Nazi organisation. But this is born of the confusion promoted by the society it-self which deliberately practises secrecy and obfuscation.

Despite the criticism of neo-Nazism and racism, the Skull and Bones society, in recent years, has set about trying to re-cruit individuals from the non-WASP ethnic groups that were once banned. Blacks, Jews, Orientals, homosexuals – all once seen as beyond the pale – are now considered for candidacy. How this is squared with the original ideas of Skull and Bones is not known. Conspiracy theorists, wondering what an elite group of wealthy WASPS would want with those they con-sider inferior, suggest that this is just a ploy to allow the even-tual re-enslavement of these groups.

Genuine criticism directed at the Skull and Bones has ar-gued that the secret society is becoming more debased, or has become too immersed in the 'occult' and has therefore become more 'evil'. It is even alleged that the society has a selection of silverware from Hitler's private collection among its ritual paraphernalia, although this remains unproven.

Once a Bonesman, always a Bonesman and the bonds that are made at Yale last a lifetime. It is often said that George Bush Jnr and Snr consulted their fellow Bonesmen for advice particularly during both Gulf wars and the power politics they involved. Henry Stimson was a man whom George Bush Snr revered and he was a great influence on the former president. Stimson maintained that a war once every generation was a healthy, spiritual event that had a cleansing effect on the nation, enabling it to rally behind a political cause. By doing this it would overcome its weaknesses in a newfound burst of patriotic fervour. The idea that combat is some kind of mystical purgative is at the heart of the Skull and Bones philosophy. But have all the wars America has fought in the latter half of the 20th century and the early 21st century been a direct result of the involvement of the Skull and Bones?

The Sufis

Sufism is a form of mysticism within Islam that often seems at odds with the teachings of the Koran, which tends to be unfavourable towards such modes of thought. Sufism came to Islam from Persia where it came under the influence of Buddhism and developed a pantheistic element. The Sufis claim their founder was a woman by the name of Rabia whose grave was situated on a hill east of Jerusalem, a place that was frequented by pilgrims in the Middle Ages. But in all likelihood it originated with one Abu-Said ibn Abi-L-Chair who set up a monastery in 815. His followers were called Sufis or '*Woollers*' from their ascetic vestments made of wool and they lived a life of contemplation, finding in pantheism a spirituality they could not find in Islam.

Not long after, Sufism divided itself into two distinct strands. The followers of the Persian Bestami, who died in 875, claimed that man was himself divine. Others followed Jonaid, another Persian, who died in 909, and were both less radical in what they believed and less vocal in expressing it.

The aim of Sufism was to destroy the passions, the baser human instincts, and thus liberate the soul so that it could be united, through love, with God from which it emanated like a ray. The more cautious Sufis were often revered as saints while the more active became martyrs. Many, for example

Hallaj, a pupil of Jonaid, who was executed in 922 by Hamid, the vizier of the Khalif Al-Moqtadir in Baghdad, became both reviled and praised in equal measure.

In Sufism the initiate must choose a mentor or teacher under whose instruction he must strive to pass through the three levels or degrees of understanding. The first is the Law – the Sufi as Muslim. The second is the Method or Way in which the Sufi practises fasting, asceticism, Sufi lore, and solitude, with occasional ventures into Hal, an ecstatic state which, when permanent, becomes known as Makam. The final level is Certainty. The objective god has now become subjective i.e. the Sufi is now god and all religion is therefore pure vanity.

Sufism is also famous for generating glorious and stunning poetry written by its adherents. Two of the most celebrated are Ferid eddin Attar who died in 1220 and Jelal eddin Rumi (1207–1273).

The Thugee

In 1816, an article appeared in the Madras Literary Gazette written by a Dr. Sherwood who had heard rumours about a mysterious secret society of assassins. This article was the first written word confirming the existence of a cult, which committed murder in the name of Kali, a Hindu Goddess who was the epitome of bloodthirstiness. She sported four arms, red eyes, was smeared with blood and gave Calcutta its name – Kali-ghat or the 'Steps of Kali'.

Thugee was a cult that worked on a hereditary membership structure and one that had the ability to transcend both caste and religion, with Hindus and Muslims both being members. Thug fathers inducted their sons into the cult's secret mysteries in their early teens. They were first taken on a Thug safari, without being told anything. On the next trip, they were told that robbery was the objective. Then they were allowed to watch a victim being strangled – a gruesome initiation. This is perhaps the only secret society ritual in which another person has to suffer actual death on behalf of the initiate. Normally initiation involves a ritualistic and faux death experience before the candidate is allowed into the order. Eventually, after experiencing the Thugee life, the initiates would acquire the rank of *bhurtote*, when they themselves were accepted as stranglers. Not all Thugs were born into the brotherhood. There was plenty of opportunity for the recruitment of outsiders, especially if they held important and powerful positions within society which could be exploited for the benefit of the cult.

Not all Kali devotees were Thugs, yet it was estimated that there were, at a conservative estimate, at least 5,000 Thugs in India at the time. The cult was said to be old, and it has been suggested that the Greek historian Herodotus, making cryptic mention of a people called the *Sagartians* who lived in central Asia, might have been referring to a source of the Thugee that was more than two thousand years old. They were said to be proficient in the arts of strangulation with a cord – something for which the Thugee or Thugs (the modern word derives from the cult) were famous.

The Thugs themselves believed that their activities were depicted in eighth-century cave temple carvings at Ellora, but such carvings have never been found and they were probably myth or story told to the cult's newer adherents. During the reign of Jalal-ud-din Khilji, the Sultan of Delhi, in the 13th century, a thousand Thugs were arrested and deported from Delhi to Bengal. Early in the next century, a leading Thug named Nizam-ud-din assisted in the repulsion of invaders from Delhi, evidence that the Thugee cult had become a powerful organisation and was a weapon of fear to be deployed at will by the ruling caste. At one stage the British discovered that high-ranking Indian bankers were involved with the cult. Through their activities the Thugee amassed great wealth – although they lived frugal, unostentatious lives – and this became a useful source of funds for bribery and other corrupt activities.

The Thugee method of killing was strangulation, from behind, using a yellow silk cloth called a *rumal*. The name *Thug* came from the Hindi verb *thaglana*, meaning 'to deceive', and refers to the subtle ability of the Thugs to befriend their intended victims and to lure them into a false sense of security (there is a similarity to the methods employed by the Assassins). More often than not this was achieved by posing as travelling merchants looking for security in numbers. With groups of murderous bandits like the *Pindari* busy waylaying the unwary, the roads in India were desperately perilous at the best of times and fearful travellers were only too happy to have the company. The disguised Thugs would then travel with their victims for long periods of time, earning trust and friendship in equal measure. Should any suspicions be aroused along the way, the Thugs often used backup groups who would join the travellers further on down the road in an attempt to assuage the fears of the intended victims. The Thugs had also developed *Ramasee*, a secret language, which enabled them to talk openly in the company of strangers.

Thugs often repeatedly used certain groves, called *beles*, to carry out their murders. When that location was reached, every Thug would conveniently position themselves around their prey. A secret command was said and, with lethal efficiency, the Thugs swiftly and silently garrotted the victim from behind. Once the bodies were picked clean of valuables, the remains were dumped in pre-dug graves. They would cut deep gashes in the bodies to hasten decomposition and thereby reduce the likelihood that jackals or other carrion-eaters would find and uncover the evidence.

The power of the Thugee began to fall away when the British, particularly under Sir William Henry Sleeman (1788–1856) set about bringing the order to heel. The Thugs proved difficult to suppress, at least initially. Once individual Thugee were captured and forced to reveal the whereabouts of their fellows, the cult began to lose its power as members, assuming that Kali had abandoned them, began to give up in droves. Soon the cult was all but extinguished, although the rumours persisted that secret enclaves still existed throughout India.

The Triads

In China secret societies have achieved a highly polished and expertly structured continuity – none more so than the Triads. It is commonly believed that they began as a resistance movement to the Manchu emperors but this is now considered to be a myth. The Manchu, hailing from Manchuria, were seen as foreign rulers, who captured China's northern capital of Peking and established their dynasty there around 1674. In the thirteen-year of rule of Kiang Hsi, the second Manchu emperor, a monastery of fighting monks called the *Siu Lam* were recruited by him to defeat a rebellion in Fukien. As a reward, the monasteries received some imperial power but, subsequently, these Fukien Buddhist monks were considered a threat and an army was sent to suppress them. Eighteen monks escaped the onslaught and only five eventually survived. These five were thought to have founded five monasteries, and five secret societies, dedicated to overthrowing the Manchu (also known as the Ch'ing) dynasty. The secret societies, longing for the golden age of Chinese history, set about restoring the previous Chinese Ming dynasty, employing a motto of 'Crush the Ch'ing, establish the Ming'.

The Ming emperors' family name was 'Hung', and used the colour red for recognition purposes. These Chinese secret societies became associated with both the name Hung (meaning 'flood') and the colour red, and called themselves the 'Hung Mun'. They developed secret codes, mainly as a way of frustrating the emperor's spies, but eventually this secrecy, and their intense martial arts training, led to the secret society being used for criminal purposes, instead of political ones. Despite this shift in emphasis the Hung Mun were still seen as protectors of the people against the emperor's brutal regime.

Over the following century these secret societies became involved in a number of rebellions against the Manchus, notably the *White Lotus Society* rebellion in Szechuan, *Hupeh* and *Shansi* in the mid-1790s; the *Cudgels* in Kwangsi province from 1847 to 1850 and the *Hung Hsiu Chuan's* Kwangsi-based rebellion between 1851 and 1865. The Boxer Rebellion in Peking between 1896 and 1900 involved the White Lotus Society along with the *Big Swords* and the *Red Fists*. Sun Yat Sen, the founder of Republican China, was allied with the *Hsing Chung* triad society, in his 1906 rebellion. Later the Triads fought the Communists while the West used the *Green Tang* to assist in this fight.

During World War Two, after the Japanese invasion, the Triads offered to work for them. The invaders united the gangs under an association called the *Hing Ah Kee Kwan* (Asia Flourishing Organisation) in order to bring them under greater control. The secret societies were used to help 'police' the residents and to suppress any anti-Japanese activity.

Following World War Two, the Communists became a Triad target again but they were ruthless in their attempted extermination of the secret societies. It was estimated that in 1947 there were 300,000 Triad members in Hong Kong alone but, when Mao Tse Tung's communists were eventually victorious in 1949, the Triads dispersed to Hong Kong, Macao, Thailand, San Francisco, Vancouver, and Perth in Australia where they still operate.

Unlike the notion that Freemasonry or the supposed Illuminati are behind certain events, the machinations of the Chinese secret societies are very much historical fact.

Other Secret Societies

Secret societies are not just the preserves of white western males. Many other cultures initiate members into elite groups. In the indigenous tribes of Australia and Africa this takes the form of tribal secrets and ancient rites that are given to the young men when they pass through ceremonies that bring them into adulthood. In Melanesia, for example, secret societies abound. The Banks Islands are home to the *Sukwe* who are based in villages and meet in a 'club house', whereas the *Tamate*, or 'ghost society' hold their clandestine meetings in the bush. One of the interesting features of the *Tamate* is the ritualistic death of a novice and rebirth into the society. In Polynesia most secret societies such as the *Kaioi* (Marquesas) or the *Areoi* (Tahiti) are connected to rituals in which young men become warriors.

In North America, secret societies of the indigenous peoples were often connected with mysteries of a religious nature and included dramatisations of myths. Others were devoted to medicine or war. In a variation on membership through an initiation rite, some societies could be entered by marriage into the tribe. In South America, initiation to an elite is through the use of extreme ordeals to test the courage of the candidate.

In Africa, in the past particularly, secret societies have been in three main areas: the extreme west beyond Liberia, Nigeria and the Congo. Most of these fall into three distinct groups – initiation societies such as the *Labi* of the Baya Tribe, those connected with the dead like the *Oro* of Yoruba, and the religious such as the *Imandwa* of Ruanda. Some African secret societies, such as the *Poro* of the Mendi, *Ogboni* of the Yoruba and the *Egbo* of the Calabar have developed along political lines. In Sierra Leone there is the women-only *Bundu* while, in the Mpongwe, women have a secret society whose main objective is to protect their sisters from male abuse. Common to a number of African orders is the use of secret language and signs. The *Poro* and the *Egbo* protect their property with the use of physical signals such as a miniature broom to ward off trespassers.

It is clear that all secret societies, whether in Masonic lodges in a town high street or tribal huts in the heart of Polynesia, have great similarities. The same progression takes place – proof of worthiness is followed by initiation and the leaving of the profane world by a staged rebirth to reappear in one where one has supposed elite status and where secret or special knowledge is learnt.

Conclusions

Secret societies have played a part in human affairs since civilisation began but how influential they are and just how deep that influence goes is a matter of conjecture and fierce debate. Groups of like-minded, often powerful people, predominantly male, will always congregate together to dress up and utter oaths of allegiance to each other for some idealistic cause. Should they be feared? What control do they really have? They have only the power which we choose to give them and mostly that is imaginary. Undoubtedly there is evidence that groups like the Bilderberg do influence world affairs but is it always for the detriment? Maybe, just maybe, they achieve things that are for the greater good. All that the critics highlight is the supposedly evil. In reality nothing is good and bad – it is all shades of grey.

As an antidote to paranoia one must always strive to look at the bigger picture. Some conspiracy theorists believe that everything we do, think or see is controlled by one secret cabal or another. Depending on the political leanings of the theorist, these cabals are either made up of left-wing subversives in league with Jewish Zionists or of right-wing, power-mad, oil-loving globalists. If one goes looking for the devil, one will find the devil. Researchers find what they are looking for. Texe Marrs, for example, is looking for satanists at work and in the spurious organisation known as the Illuminati he finds them.

Most of the accusations laid at the door of secret societies are plain wrong and tell us more about the accuser than the accused. Certainly secret societies look after their own but is that not done in all levels of society, in all kinds of social groups? Critics often harbour their own prejudices, which taint their perceptions. From certain quarters the attacks are nothing more than thinly disguised anti-Semitism; from another direction the criticisms are simply delusional paranoia. In some cases it is simple jealousy.

If there does turn out to be a hidden pattern in the streets of Washington DC, patterns that include an Illuminati owl, the obvious reply is 'So what?' If L'Enfant, one of the city's designers, was obsessed with occult geometry this does not make it any more real than if the head of Homer Simpson was discovered to be a pattern used by the Stonecutters for street layouts in Springfield. As often happens, great weight is attached to something vacuous and empty, dragging with it ill-conceived notions about the world.

In terms of hidden knowledge the real 'secrets of the universe' are those being highlighted and discovered by science. All the knowledge that humanity has gleaned about the world has come through study, experimentation, learning, measurement and logic. No 'divine rites' have given us glimpses into quantum mechanics or brought us the cure for cancer or the structure of DNA.

If there is genuine criticism to be aimed at secret societies, ridiculous theories about lizards disguised as humans and the like serve only to muddy the waters. The Christian right see the devil at work in lodges and sanctum sanctorums up and down the land but they are just as misguided as those who maintain that secret societies cover up the so-called 'reality' of flying saucers, the moon landings or the Holy Grail. One group known as *The Aviary* – because all its members have secret bird names – claim extraterrestrials have holographic images of the crucifixion. Why holograms? Why not something far more advanced? These ETs, according to the Aviary, also claim that they are awaiting the fourth horseman of the apocalypse. Do ETs have ideas based on the Bible? The answer is they do not. Equally daft is the idea of the *Cult of the Serpent* in which it is claimed that NASA has been working with lizard entities to turn the world into some socialist nightmare via (by some means) space exploration. Such stories, tainted by delusion and a religious zeal, have their origins in all-too-human credulity and gullibility.

If critics delude themselves with stories of lizards and extraterrestrials, then those guilty of crimes against humanity slip through the net. Without doubt there are those who wish to control the world's resources and ideologies, using whatever means are at their disposal. Whether they are members of a lodge, or worship owls is almost incidental.

If the activities of a particular country's government are wrong, then we should accuse it of deceit, not shadowy cadres of men bent on 'devil worship'. It is the power base that must account for itself and it is misguided, to say the least, to accuse those in power simply because they happen to be Freemasons or are guests of the Bilderberg Group. Did Freemasonry bring down Enron or was it simple old-fashioned greed?

Throughout history secret societies have come and gone, have claimed much but have sunk without trace. Some would argue that secret societies are the repositories of information that church and state would rather have us forget. But what kind of information? That Jesus might have been married and had children? Is this so earth-shattering? Careful consideration of the so-called 'secrets' reveals that, in all cases, that which is secret is vacuous and inconsequential. While people continue to believe in false notions such as Atlantis, creationism, the Face on Mars, alien abduction, ESP, the Bermuda Triangle, the Bible Code, the Loch Ness Monster and thousands of other weird ideas, they will also believe that secret societies are the root cause of all kinds of problems.

Do secret societies really operate behind the curtain? If that curtain was pulled back, what would be revealed? The world is a dangerous and risky place as it is. Economies rise and fall, companies are taken over or collapse, house prices rise then plummet and the weather wrecks crops, oil prices, countries and the stock market. Institutions suffer from political infighting, crime rates increase, sure-fire hit films flop at the box office, leaders mess up, terrorist groups flourish, soldiers kill the wrong people, plagues lay waste to populations. It is mindless paranoia to place the blame on secret societies and hidden conspiracies. If AIDS came from a CIA test tube, as some claim, does that mean the Black Death that wiped out most of Europe in the 14th century was born from some experiments by an apocalyptic Christian cult? If we are all due to have illicit micro-chip implants to control us, as some theorists believe, just how long will it take to implant six billion people and what will be the cost? Just how does the New World Order intend to do this? It is difficult to get a consensus on minor issues between two people let alone in an undertaking of this magnitude. The fear and paranoia must be outweighed by reason and a proper grasp of reality.

We have more to fear from general ignorance of the world than from the apparent machinations of secret societies with their bizarre handshakes and passwords. Events in the world are manipulated, as undoubtedly they are, for profit not for the grand ideals of secret societies. Secret societies are just a sideshow or a distraction. We are foolish to believe in secret knowledge and we are foolish to believe the conspiracy theorists and their hysterical notions of devil-run secret cadres plotting our enslavement or to put faith in the insidious anti-Semitic ideologies that underpin many of the theories. As Michael Shermer writes in his excellent *Why People Believe Weird Things*, 'For the conspiratorialist, all manner of demonic forces have been at work throughout history, including, of course, the Jews, but also the Illuminati, Knights Templar, Knights of Malta, Masons, Freemasons, Cosmopolitans, Abolitionists, Slaveholders, Catholics, Communists, Council on Foreign Relations, Trilateral Commission, Warren Commission, World Wildlife Fund, International Monetary Fund, League of Nations, United Nations and many more … In many of these, "the Jews" are seen to be at work behind the scenes.' Ultimately this distracts from genuine criticism of those who do determine our futures.

In the end, secret societies do not stay secret very long and the 'secret rulers of the world' prove to be, like everyone else, riddled with human frailties, failings and fears. Yet, when Grovers, Illuminati and the Skull and Bones members attend their secret meetings, they may very well be having a laugh up their collective sleeves. What gives secret societies their presumed power is not so much the society itself but the outside world's perception of it. Secret societies may be guilty of playing on the fears and suspicions of non-members and using it to their advantage but, in the final analysis, they are guardians of an empty room.

If a mysterious super-elite secret society really ran the world so completely, then no voice of dissent would ever be heard and there are plenty of those. When we realise that secret societies have no secrets and little real control then their power is diminished. It is all about perception and nothing more.

If powerful men decide to exercise their will undemocratically and behind closed doors – and there is much evidence to suggest that is exactly what they are doing – then they should be criticised. But when misinformed individuals talk of the devil, satanism, 12-foot high lizards, owl worship, divine secrets and extraterrestrials showing us holograms of mythical events, the criticism plunges into the realm of the deeply trivial and serves neither the individual nor society at large.

*

The French have an expression: '*Un secret de Polichinelle*'. Polichinelle is the French equivalent of Punch. In the old puppet shows his secrets are told to the audience as stage whispers and are therefore not secret at all.

Bibliography

Baigent, Michael, Leigh, Richard and Lincoln, Henry, *The Holy Blood and The Holy Grail,* London: Jonathan Cape, 1982

Baigent, Michael, Leigh, Richard and Lincoln, Henry, *The Messianic Legacy,* London: Jonathan Cape, 1986

Baigent, Michael and Leigh, Richard, *The Temple and the Lodge*, London: Jonathan Cape, 1989

Bartlett, W.B., *The Assassins: The Story of Islam's Medieval Secret Sect*, Stroud: Sutton Publishing, 2001

Brown, Dan, *The Da Vinci Code,* London: Bantam, 2003

Colquoun, Ithell, *Sword of Wisdom*, London: Neville Spearman, 1975

DaRaul, Arkon, *Secret Societies: A History,* New York: MJF Books, 1989

Eringer, Robert, *The Global Manipulators,* Bristol: Pentacle Books, 1980

Fells, Richard, *A Visitor's Guide to Underground Britain*, London: Bloomsbury, 1993

Goldstein, Paul and Steinberg, Jeffrey, *George Bush, Skull & Bones and the New World Order*, International Edition White Paper, 1991

Gribbin, John, *Science: A History,* London: Penguin, 2003

Harvey, Paul (editor), *The Oxford Companion To Classical Literature,* Oxford: Oxford University Press, 1937

Kick, Russ (editor), *Everything You Know Is Wrong*, New York: The Disinformation Company, 2001

Kick, Russ (editor), *You Are Being Lied To*, New York: The Disinformation Company, 2002

Knight, Christopher and Lomas, Robert, *The Hiram Key*, London: Century, 1996

Kueshana, Eklal, *The Ultimate Frontier*, Chicago: The Stelle Group, 1974

Mannix, Daniel P., *The Hellfire Club*, London: New English Library, 1967

Martin, Sean, *The Knights Templar*, London: Pocket Essentials, 2004

McCormick, Donald, *The Hellfire Club*, London: Jarrolds, 1958

Piatigorsky, Alexander, *Who's Afraid of The Freemasons?*, London: The Harvill Press, 1997

Pilger, John, *The New Rulers of the World*, London: Verso, 2002

Seward, Desmond, *The Monks of War: The Military Religious Orders*, London: Penguin Books, 1992

Shermer, Michael, *Why People Believe Weird Things*, New York: Henry Holt and Co, 2002

Short, Martin, *Inside the Brotherhood*, London: Grafton, 1989

Towers, Eric, *Dashwood: The Man and the Myth*, Wellington, Northamptonshire: Aquarian Press, 1986

Wilgus, Neal, *The Illuminoids*, Santa Fe, New Mexico: Sun Publishing, 1978

Yallop, David, *In God's Name*, London: Jonathan Cape, 1984

On the Web

The following are of interest. There are numerous websites dedicated to secret societies but most tend towards the hysterical. In some there is a degree of anti-Semitism. Some are created from the point of view of the religious right who see nothing but the work of the devil in secret societies. Many of the websites are full of paranoia and display a lack of a functioning critical process. The author and the publisher are not responsible for the material displayed on the following.

General
www.Jimmarrs.com
www.global-conspiracies.com
www.secretsofthetomb.com
www.bilderberg.org

Æth Priesthood
http://www.bevhall.com/BHC7S.html

AMORC
http://www.amorc.org/index.shtml

Ancient Rosae Crucis, ARC
http://www.arcgl.org/index.html

Antiquae ordo Mystiquae Prieure de Sion
http://home.fireplug.net/~rshand/streams/scripts/sion.
html

Bibliography of the Knights of St. John of the Hospital
http://orb.rhodes.edu/bibliographies/st-john_bib.html

B'nai B'rith
http://bnaibrith.org/index.html

Builders of the Adytum
http://www.atanda.com/bota/

DeMolay International
http://www.demolay.org/

Eastern Star Links
http://www.mastermason.com/mmlinks/oes.htm

Ecclesia Gnostica Catholica
http://www.crl.com/~thelema/egc.html

Franciscan Order of Céli Dé
http://www.bcpl.lib.md.us/~jketler/grayfriar.html

Fraternal Order of Police Grand Lodge
http://www.grandlodgefop.org/

Fraternitas Rosae Crucis
http://home.earthlink.net/~bellaluxlabs/fraternitas.html

General Grand Chapter & Council York Rite Freemasonry
http://members.aol.com/YorkRiteFM/HomePage.html

Grand Lodge of Israel
http://www.geocities.com/Athens/Forum/9991/

Grand Lodge of New York F&AM
http://www.nymasons.org/

Grand Lodge of Scotland
http://www.grandlodgescotland.com

Bella Grotto
http://members.tripod.com/~belagrotto/JoinUs.html

Hermetic Order of the Golden Dawn
http://www.golden-dawn.com

High Royal Arch Knight Templar Priests
http://members.aol.com/YorkRiteFM/HRAKTP.html

Imperial Council, Shrine of North America
http://www.shrinershq.org/

Knights Hospitaller
http://web.mit.edu/redingtn/www/ecole/ksj.html/

Knights of Columbus Supreme Council
http://www.kofc-supreme-council.org/

Knights Templar
http://www.homeusers.prestel.co.uk/church/templars/
templars.htm

Links to Masonic Grand Lodges
http://www.nymasons.org/glsites.html

Martinist Order of the Knights of Christ
http://members.aol.com/GMTHG/omcc.html

Martinist Order of the Temple
http://members.aol.com/GMTHG/mart.html

Mevlevi Order (Dervishes)
http://www.sufism.org/threshld/society/mevlev.html

Most Venerable Order of the Hospital of Saint John of Jerusalem
http://www.saintjohn.org/

Nimatullah Order
http://www.anglia.ac.uk/~trochford/glossary/sufi/
nimatull.html

O A I
http://www.tgd.org/oai/

Order of the Mystic Christ
http://www.ica.org.au/5.html

Ordo Templi Orientis U.S. Grand Lodge
http://www.otohq.org/

Philalethes Society
http://www.Freemasonry.org/psoc/

Phylaxis Society – Prince Hall
http://www.geocities.com/Athens/Acropolis/2704/

Poor Knights of Christ and of the Temple of Solomon
http://www.homeusers.prestel.co.uk/church/templars/templars.htm

Red Cross of Constantine
http://members.aol.com/YorkRiteFM/RCC.html

Religious and Military Order of Knights of the Holy Sepulchre of Jerusalem
http://members.tripod.com/~Baron91/ohs.html

Rosicrucian Order, AMORC
http://www.rosicrucian.org/

Rosicrucian Order AMORC Worldwide
http://www.amorc.org/

Rosy Cross
http://www.bevhall.com/BHC6S.html

Royal Order of Scotland
http://members.aol.com/YorkRiteFM/ROS.html

Sovereign Military Hospitaller Order of Saint John of Jerusalem of Rhodes and of Malta
http://www.chivalricorders.org/chivalric/smom/malta.htm

St. John – Other Orders
http://www.smom.org/other/index.html

Sovereign Order of the Orthodox Knights Hospitaller of Saint John of Jerusalem
http://members.tripod.com/~OstJ/index.html

Supreme Bethel International Order of Job's Daughters
http://www.iojd.org/

Supreme Council 33° Ancient Accepted Scottish Rite Freemasonry Northern Jurisdiction
http://world.std.com/~sysmgr

Supreme Council 33° Ancient Accepted Scottish Rite Freemasonry Northern Jurisdiction (Back Door)
http://www.supremecouncil.org

Supreme Council 33° Ancient Accepted Scottish Rite Freemasonry Southern Jurisdiction
http://www.srmason-sj.org/index.html

Templar Knights
http://home.mem.net/~babech/TEMPLAR.htm

Temple of Isis – Mighty Mother
http://www.golden-dawn.org/

Temple of the Holy Grail
http://members.aol.com/GMTHG/thg.html

Thelemic Order of the Golden Dawn
http://www.tgd.org/

Thule Net
http://thulenet.com/

Index

THE BREATH OF GOD, HIS WORD AND FIAT.

YOB FILIAE

The Ancient and Mystical Order

Rosae Crucis